BE CAREFUL WHAT YOU CLICK FOR

A Girlfriend's Guide to Online Mating

By

Diane L. Roberts

Own Publications

www.carefulwhatyouclickfor.com

This book is a work of non-fiction. All information and opinions expressed herein are the views of the author. This publication is intended to provide accurate and authoritative information concerning the subject matter covered and is for informational purposes only. Neither the author nor the publisher is attempting to provide legal advice of any kind.

BE CAREFUL WHAT YOU CLICK FOR: A Girlfriend's Guide to Online Mating.
© 2010 by Diane L. Roberts
All Rights Reserved
Cover Design by Diane L. Roberts
© 2011 All Rights Reserved

ISBN-13: 978-1470100056
ISBN-10: 1470100053

First publication: September 2011 (Black Opal Books)
Second publication: February 2012 (Own Publications)

Copyright US, Reg #TXu 1-771-843, August 22, 2011
Copyright CAN, Reg #1081974, November 9, 2010

"But what if I fall in love with Mr. Right for One Night?"
"Oh man, I think I just met a Rusty Corolla Dude. Now what?"
"How can I spot a Penis with Potential?"

It may seem like a foreign language, but if you're looking for love online, you will need to be able to speak it, and you'll need to know the answers. CLICK will tell you the truth about the ups and downs, frustrations and realities of the erratic world of online dating.

Ready to give up? Don't. Ten years, over thirty-six thousand e-mails, flirts, smiles, and winks, hundreds of phone conversations and coffee dates, even a relationship or two – like millions, Diane has been there, done that, and everything you'll learn is based on her own experience.

Nobody else in the online dating world is going to tell you about the three-point disability, how to spot the defect and return the goods, or how to deal with a borderline boy--- but Diane will. Meet higher quality men, and take charge of your online dating experiences, starting now.

Millions of women are looking for love online. The competition is fierce, and you need an edge. So grab that mouse, take charge of your destiny, and let's get CLICKing.

DEDICATION

To Bonnie Hearn Hill
You listened to me, laughed with me, then told me to write this book.
It never would have happened without you.

I am forever grateful.

INTRODUCTION

Internet dating sites in the US raked in over $495 million back in 2005. That number continues to increase every year, and according to one study, is expected to climb to over $900 million by the end of 2011. Aside from pornography, internet dating services are the biggest paid content segment on the web. Thirty-one percent of adults in America (about 47 million people) say they know someone who has used an Internet dating service. If you're reading this book, my guess is you are one of them.

So, the odds of finding your soul mate must be good, right? Think again. You can "Mind, Find, Bind," eHarmonize, or Plenty-o-Fish yourself to death, if you don't accept the fact that, to a great extent, you're dealing with the substandard, you'll be disappointed.

I know you're thinking, "Hey, Diane, I'm not substandard, and I'm on those sites. What's up with that?"

The short answer is you're right. A lot of the women aren't substandard at all, but you're not looking for a woman, are you?

Is he out there? Possibly. Want to find him before you're 150 years old? Keep reading.

After receiving more than 36,000 emails, flirts, smiles and winks, and going on too many dates to count, I'm going to walk you through the insane world of online mating. Some of this will make you laugh. Some will make you cry. Some will make you want to pull your hair out. Oh, and trust me, the older you are, the more hair you are going to lose, so be prepared to buy a wig.

A friend of mine convinced me to try it after I ended a three-year relationship with a man who, (surprise, surprise) turned out to be married. What's worse, he got married while we were involved in a long distance relationship. Go figure...the creep *forgot* to tell me. After that, I decided why not? It wasn't as if meeting a man in person meant he'd be a higher quality person, right?

Still, I worried, just as every online novice does. What if nobody responded to my ad? Hello! After posting my profile and receiving more than 200 messages in the first week, I realized, not only was I crazy for being worried about not getting a reply, but that I was more attractive to a lot more men than I thought I was. Cool.

The Internet really opened up my world, or I should say opened my eyes to the world. Why was I limiting myself to men who lived in the same city? Especially if I was willing to relocate if I found the man of my dreams.

Through all my trials and tribulations, I have met some great people and made some long-term friends. Like anything, though, there's the good, the bad and the ugly, and we'll be talking about how to spot and avoid those last two right away.

This book is going to make you think of online dating in a whole new way, and trust me, you'll be able to find your Mr. Right much faster when you learn what I learned from ten years of clicking. First, we'll cover the basics including creating profiles men will respond to. Then I'll drill two very simple rules into your head – the caveman rules. You'll learn why it's important to set standards and stick to them in order to avoid the "at least he's..." Then we'll wade through the shit together. It's not that bad, and we'll be out of there before you know it.

I am assuming, if you're reading this, you're looking for a serious relationship, and that you are a straight woman looking for a straight man.

"But, Diane, if I do everything you say, I'll never have a date again."

Wrong! You'll never have *a bad relationship* again. You'll never sit by the phone waiting for a call from Thick11 again. You'll never sleep with BootyDaddy7 and then regret it. You'll still have bad dates, but at least you'll recognize the signs, and be able to end it before it's gone too far. You'll still sleep with men, if you want to, but at least you'll know why you did it and what to expect after the fact. This book will lay it out for you. Nothing in here, including the language, is nicey-nicey. If you're not offended by an occasional fuck (and I mean that both literally and figuratively), and you're willing to change your approach to meeting men online—then, let's get clicking

TABLE OF CONTENTS

CHAPTER 1

IT'S ALL ABOUT YOU

J **ust post it, princess, post it:**
In order to be found, you're going to have to advertise the fact ~~that you're a desperate, lonely woman who can't find love and has therefore resorted to the Internet~~ that your beautiful, luscious, self is available.

Okay, I already know what you're thinking, and I want you to stop right now. There is no need for any trepidation about posting a profile and your photo.

"I'm not going to Internet date. What if everyone finds out? Won't they think I'm a desperate loser?"

Uhm, no. If "everyone" is surfing the Internet, specifically, dating websites, most of which require them to register to even do a search, looking for you, then I hate to say it, but that makes them the losers.

Second, who is "everyone?" Your friends? Family? Co-workers? Think about it. Everyone you know who is married doesn't do this. If, however, your best friend's husband finds you on Match.com then something is wrong with him, not you. Get my drift?

Those who might happen to see your profile are probably on the site themselves. It's not nice for the pot to call the kettle black now is it?

DIANE SAYS: I understand that that some professional or high profile people feel uncomfortable with the idea of posting their photo. All I can say is – if you don't post a photo you're not going to get the volume or the type of responses you need and want. As such you may need to consider a different dating venue.

Let's get back to the sites.

There are so many niche dating services and sites now, there's no reason to go with the mainstream ones if, for example, you are passionate about something, and hope to share that passion with someone in a relationship.

Vegetarian?	Greenfriends.com or
	Veggiedate.com
Hearing impaired?	Deafs.com
Horse lover?	Equestriancupid.com
Farmer?	Farmersonly.com

Big and beautiful?	Largefriends.com or Bigcupid.com
Jewish?	Jdate.com or Jewishcafe.com
Star Trek freak?	Trekpassions.com
Have an STD?	PositiveSingles.com
Love bikers?	Bikerkiss.com
Over the age of 50?	Seniorfriendfinder.com
Golf nut?	Golfmates.com
Gold digger?	Millionairematch.com or Sugardaddy.com
Christian?	Christiancupid.com or Christianmingle.com
Goth?	Gothicmatch.com

The possibilities are endless, so don't be afraid to search around and find a site that works for you. Obviously, I've only listed the ones who agreed to pay me to put them in my book—I wish.

Before we talk about photos, I want to make sure you understand that some sites are specifically designed for "intimate encounters" (i.e. the "I wanna meet yah and bang yah for one night" site). Please stay away from these sites if you're serious about finding a relationship. There is a lot of old thinking out there, and it all boils down to: "If he sleeps with me, then he's my boyfriend." Wrong, wrong, wrong!

No matter what site you meet him on, a guy is not your boyfriend until he introduces you to all his close friends and family as such. This is unlikely to happen with a girl he's met on one of those sites. All he'll be thinking about after his encounter with you is, "See yah." Then he'll tuck in his shirt and hike it out of there.

Something else you might need to know is, and I bring this up because I've experienced it personally, the more expensive the site is to join, it seems, the shorter, fatter, balder and uglier the men will be. Why? I'm guessing they aren't making the cut on the mainstream sites and have gravitated towards those who claim to offer more for the money, for example, better matches, better matching criteria, and higher success rates. The point here is, don't believe that just because a guy is willing to pay a higher price to be on a particular site, that he's any better than a guy you can find on any other site.

Okay, now that you've gotten over your fear of posting a photo of yourself holding a cucumber in a provocative way on Farmersonly.com (just kidding), let's talk about those photos.

The Right Photo Is Worth a Thousand Clicks:

If you want to have profile savvy, listen up. Your photos are the most important part of your profile. Men will scroll through photos of women tirelessly, clicking on the ones that appeal to them. Do exactly what I suggest and you will increase your profile traffic ten-fold.

You must have at least three, good quality, clear, recent, photos of yourself. They should be as follows:

- 1 nice head shot, clearly showing your face, hair, and fabulous smile.

- 1 full-length shot of you in casual clothes. Keep it simple: jeans and a nice top.

- 1 full-length shot of you in a dress. This dress should be sleeveless, low cut but not showing more than 1-inch of cleavage, and it should also show your legs. Above the knee is totally fine. If you've got 'em flaunt 'em, but don't, whatever you do, wear a mini or micro-mini. This is the photo you will use for your profile photo.

Did you know that in some countries, women over 35 are put to death for wearing a mini skirt? Okay, that's not true, but "What Not to Wear" says it's a big no, no. Unless you want them to show up at your door with a camera crew, dig out something else.

A serious, relationship-minded man is going to be looking for someone he believes he could introduce to his family one day. Don't post booty shots, too much cleavage, or clothing that belongs on a 16-year-old (unless you are 16 years old).

You know what? I take that back. Go ahead and post those booty shots, but don't expect a second date. You'll be bombarded with trollers, guys who are married, or want nothing but smut talk on MSN or a one-night stand. If you're okay with being on the speed dial list along with your booty shot counterparts, have'at'er.

How recent?

If they are more than 2-years-old, or your weight has changed by 10 pounds (more or less), then throw them away and start over. If you don't have at least three wonderful, recent photos of yourself, showing your accurate weight and size, then get someone to help you take them. Cameras are cheap, and even low-priced digital cameras can be purchased for under fifty bucks. Everyone has a friend, sister, co-worker, daughter, cousin or someone who can take a few photos for them. If you're afraid to confess why you need the photos, then invest ten more bucks and get the camera with a self-timer. Whatever you do, do not, I repeat, do not take photos of yourself with a cell phone in the bathroom mirror – or any other mirror for that matter. We're going to be talking about deleting profiles of men who do this so please don't do it yourself.

Why the dress, Diane?

Simple. Men love skin. They are visual. Hence strip clubs, Playboy Magazine, and those cheap-ass pens that you can get in Las Vegas where you flip it over and the girl's bathing suit drops down.

That photo will be your profile photo, and it needs to be exactly as I described. Classy. With skin.

Why two full-length photos?

I'm going to make this easy for you. When you go shopping for a dress, often what you do is walk along the street or inside the mall and check out the mannequins in the window.

If you see one in a dress you like, you are very likely to go in and try that dress on. Aren't you? We all know that's why stores have window displays.

Think of your profile as a window display and what you want is only the men who like what they see to come into your store and try you on. Get what I'm saying here?

Don't worry about your thighs, your belly, your chin, your arms, your lips.

There are millions of men out there, and not all of them want Pamela Anderson. If they did, then Internet porn would be boring—but guess what—I've looked and it's not!

There are sites for big boobs, small boobs, school girls, mothers, light skin, dark skin, shaved bush, full bush – the list goes on and on. The preferences are endless so why struggle with it?

Date men who are attracted to you, the real you, the you they are actually going to see when you meet them for coffee.

It's called "free text" not a free-for-all:

Ever heard the saying, "Keep it simple, stupid"? If yes, good. If not, you have now.

What you say in the free text portion of your profile needs to be simple. Don't overload men with your all your hopes, dreams, opinions, sad stories, or any other drama. You aren't on the site to whine and moan about your past. You're there to find your future.

Keep it brief, airy, happy, and fresh. Most men don't read it anyway. They set their search criteria then make a two-second decision based on your profile photo. How can you tell how long he spent on you before he reacted? This is a pretty good rule of thumb.

- If he sends you a "flirt," "wink," or "smile" it's unlikely he read your profile. He probably just reacted to your photo. Not always a bad sign, but a truly interested man will like your photo then read your profile to find something in it he can comment on, for example he might say, *"Hey, I noticed you're a consultant, I am too."* This is the man you should respond to.

Back to brief, airy, and happy. Let's look at a couple real examples of what NOT to say:

"TEXT MESSAGING HAS MADE MEN LAZY. IT IS VERY IMPERSONAL! WHY DO I PREFER OLDER MEN? THIS IS WHY. THEY KEEP IT OLD SCHOOL!

IF I GIVE YOU MY F*C*ING NUMBER AND YOU TEXT ME, YOU'RE HISTORY."

Wow, she even took the time to put it all in caps. I guess swearing wasn't emphasis enough. Comes off just a tad angry, doesn't it? If you were a guy, would you want to respond to an ad like this? I didn't think so. All right, all right, I can't help myself, another nit-pick on this one, "you are" history is "you're" history not "your" history. If you're going to put it all in caps, make darn sure it's write, I mean right.

"I love me, I adore me, I respect me, I cherish me, I am proud of me. I care about me. Now it's all about me. I am not conceited. I am just loving me…"

Believe it or not, the profession of self-love continues beyond that, I cut it short for your sake. All right, I understand exercises in self-esteem, but this isn't a place to practice your affirmations. It's a dating website, not Sedona. Put yourself in his shoes. If I were the guy reading this, I'd be thinking, *"Man, she sure doesn't need me to love her, she's got it going on all by herself."* Indeed. Hence her relationship status.

"I will be your next stalker (just kidding) or am I wooooooooo"

Don't ever joke about something like this. Never. If I were a guy, I'd be clicking as fast as I could to get to the next profile. My advice to her – delete this immediately and don't quit your day job. Joan Rivers you are not.

"Honestly, does anyone really care all that much.....is it only about if they like what they see...and then nine times out of ten what I

say won't be remembered. It's all a bit crazy. But I'm not mad at you. It is what it is. I've learned that you can't make someone like you, love you, or believe in you. Maybe God has allowed our paths to cross for some reason. One thing I will say about myself is that if someone takes the time to get to know me you will either love me or hate me......but most people love me......someday everything will all make perfect sense, so for now, laugh at confusion, smile through the tears, and keep reminding yourself that everything happens for a reason."

Oh please, wake me up when this is over. What's crazy about this is she already knows it isn't being read nine times out of ten, so why did she write all that? Boring. She's right. Guys don't read this stuff.

Here are some more simple no-nos:

- *I am looking for love, marriage and children.*

Eek. Reading that made me nervous. Imagine how a guy will feel.

- *My ex-boyfriend is a jerk, and I don't want to meet someone just like him.*

Step right up. You can be the next contestant on *Who's My Jerk?*

- *I am looking for a lifelong commitment.*

Come on now. You know men are allergic to that word.

- *I am willing to relocate.*

This might be true, but don't say it in your profile. It screams desperation. The poor guy will get this vision of you and your three kids showing up in his driveway with a U-Haul. Can he click next any faster?

> • *I don't believe this will work, but I'm trying it anyway.*

Well hello, Miss Congeniality, shall I pour a whole pile of my energy into trying to convince you that it will? Nawh, forget about it SUZIEQ23 over here seems like she's a little easier to please.

> • *The man I want to meet is a sophisticated professional. He's compassionate, driven, handsome, fit, rich, not a liar, not a cheat. He loves the outdoors, loves children, and isn't cheap.*

Let me see if I have this right. So what you're saying is, you want to meet a man who doesn't exist?

All right, so we've covered some of the don't-do-it stuff. Let's see an example of a brief, airy, happy, and fresh profile. Here's all you need to say, just three simple sentences:

I am a positive, upbeat professional. I enjoy water sports, hiking and fine dining. I hope to meet someone with similar interests.

Here's a template you can use. Just fill in the blanks, 1 word per blank:

I am a *(insert 3 positive words that describe you)*

_____, _____, _____.

I enjoy *(insert 3 activities that you enjoy doing)*

———————————, ———————————, ———————————.

I hope to meet someone with similar interests.

There, you're done. Spellcheck it then go and post it. If a guy is interested in knowing more about you, he will ask. That's what the email functionality on the site is for. Trust me. You won't get fewer responses to your profile if you use the three-sentence technique. It's all about the skin girlfriend, the skin.

Will you have him at hello?

Thankfully, women aren't nearly as bad with this as men are. I've never seen a TIGHTVAGINA4U, or BIGTITTYKITTY, but then again, maybe I haven't looked hard enough. So I don't think we need another template. We'll just take a quick look at a few that could be better:

- MISSINGMYHELP – Great, just what a guy wants - to know he'll have to financially support or be the step baby-daddy before he's even read your profile. This is not "how to lose a man in 10 clicks," it's your life. Get your thinking cap out and come up with something that will attract men, not repel them.

- JUICYAZHOTTIE – Come on now, you can do better than this. Even AZHOTTIE is better. JUICY just takes it down a road we don't need to be going down.

- SPOILED1969 – It's all about first impressions and I'm not sure "get out your wallet" is the right one to make. This might be okay if you're stunning looking, have a body like Halle Berry's, and you're on Sugardaddy.com. Nawh, probably not. Even then men are likely to just be figuring out if the booty is worth the $ or not.

All that other stuff they ask you for:

As you know, many websites require you to fill out their helpful little checklists where all you have to do it put a tick mark beside everything you like – wind surfing, horse-drawn carriage rides, romantic walks on the beach, blah, blah, blah. Sure, you love to do that stuff, and that's great, but seriously? Most men will not take the time to read your profile. For them it's all about the photo and the skin, and now that you've got profile savvy, you know this. So, don't waste a whole lot of time digging deep to come up with stuff you think will help you find a better man, because it won't. Following the delete rules in Chapter #3 will help you come up with a better man, and we'll get there soon enough.

For the rest of all that other stuff they ask you for, here's an easy-to-follow checklist.

- DON'T submit long checklists. Choose the "rather not say" option. If it forces you to answer, chose a maximum of three.

- DON'T say you are stunning looking unless at least three of your friends will agree with you in writing. It's not because you aren't, it's because there's something endearing about being just a tad humble. Go with "very good looking" or whatever the choice is that is one level down from the top.

- DON'T post photos of your sister, cousin or anyone other than yourself.

- DON'T post head shots only. Guys will immediately think you're doing this because you are fat. Give them the opportunity to decide for themselves what is or isn't too heavy for their tastes.

- DO be honest about your height, weight, and/or body shape.

- DON'T reveal your real income, or income range. Again, chose the rather-not-say option. Until the two of you are talking marriage, it's none of his business.

- DO be honest about your kids, but do not, whatever you do, post photos of under age children. Seriously. It's wrong.

- DON'T answer questions that require a negative answer, e.g. what is your worst habit?

- DO understand that your profile is a first impression. Don't ruin what could be an opportunity for a decent relationship by starting it off with a lie.

Now that you are over your fear of posting a profile, know what kinds of sites appeal to you, and understand exactly what kinds of photos to post, you're way ahead of the pack. Also, you won't be scaring men away with needy, rambling or demanding language, and you absolutely know that it's okay to tell the truth about your weight. That said, you should be ready to move to the next step. But wait, first you have to agree to the following.

Diane, I am looking for a real relationship. Therefore, I promise I will not:

☐   Worry about what *everyone else* thinks about my choice to go online.

☐   Lie about how good my sexy body looks or how much I weigh. I've got it, and I'm going to flaunt it in a classy way.

☐   Attract trollers by posting booty call photos.

☐   Waffle on about previous relationships, swear, or suggest I might be his next stalker x-girlfriend.

☐   Wear a micro-mini if I'm over 35.

☐   Think it's a good idea to use an intimate encounters site or section to snag a man.

☐   Be the next BIGTITTYKITTY.

Your autograph please:

_____

All right then, you're now ready for reality. Let's keep clickin'.

CHAPTER 2

A CAVEMAN AND A COUPLE OF PRINCESSES

The Caveman Rules:

All right, you survived Chapter 1, and now you're ready to memorize the caveman rules. Great. Just remember, if you don't learn these rules, you'll never get off the booty call list. The beauty of them is, they're simple, and that means there are no excuses. Repeat after me:

<u>#1 – Boy hunts girl down.</u>

There is NO exception to this rule.

<u>#2 – Girl responds to boy who hunts girl down.</u>

There is NO exception to this rule either, and there are only two possible responses:

1. positive = continue to hunt me
2. negative = stop hunting me

There it is—everything you need to know. This book just paid for itself.

I'm not going to go into a long explanation of the hunter gatherer theory. You have probably heard it before. It's just a matter of reminding you and making sure you understand that this is real!

Men want to pursue you, Internet or otherwise. They like to feel as if they conquered something to get you, to win you over. That's why all the stories we read about princesses when we were growing up, ended with a prince coming to a damsel's rescue.

If you still don't want to believe me, let's review the facts.

Sleeping Beauty:

Fact: Early version written by The Brothers Grimm (men), later adapted into the popular version we all know by Walt Disney (a man).

Fact: Prince Phillip goes through hell to get to this girl. He escapes from a mountain while being attacked. Then he has to slay this chick who turns herself into a gigantic fire-breathing dragon. Then, after all that (and he never once stops for a Red Bull or anything), he climbs all the way up to Aurora's chamber, and removes the curse with a kiss! Of course it ends with the "happily ever after" dance, the way they always do.

Cinderella:

Fact: Early version written by Charles Perrault in 1697 (man), again, later adapted into the popular version we all know by Walt Disney (a man).

Fact: Poor old Prince Charming has the pick of the litter, but can't find the right maiden until Cinderella shows up. Then she disappears leaving behind a glass slipper. Intrigued, the dude schleps his way all around town trying to find the woman who fits the shoe. Again, once he finds her off they go, "happily ever after."

What's my point? Neither Sleeping Beauty nor Cinderella sent either of these guys a flirt, wink, smile or email. One slept, the other scrubbed floors, and they both got their men!

Do you want your "happily ever after" or not? These stories were created by the minds of men, and I think they are an accurate representation of how they think.

So it's simple. Let the dude chase after you, because if he's not, he's probably chasing after someone else, and that's not going to land you your, "happily ever after."

Let's move on.

Does it suck? Yes. I'm a woman, and I hate it just as much as you, but that's the way the unfair world works.

This isn't something brilliant or new. It's always been this way, like since, hmmm, let me think? The caveman days? But, for some reason, the Internet dating scene seems to only have one rule, and it's everything goes. Well guess what? I'm here to tell you, being in a virtual world does not change the need for the Caveman Rules! Not if you're serious about finding a relationship.

I know you love to analyze relationships just as much as I do, so let's look at an example right now:

> • You are in a bar, and a man you think is cute notices you but then walks away and starts talking to another woman. Do you believe he was interested, approach him anyway, and interrupt his conversation with what's-her-face? Not likely. So why the heck would you do it in cyberspace? He clearly wasn't interested enough to approach you first, or at all.

The point is (translated to the Internet) the man has to be interested enough in you, to reply to your ad.

That's not fair, Diane!

I know. Oh well. You'll get over it.

Look, I'm not saying you can't surf the sites and check out men's profiles. You definitely can. Just don't be the one to initiate contact. I know this is killing you, so here's how you can take more control of the situation:

> • <u>Who Viewed Me</u>? – You've probably noticed that most sites have a feature that shows both parties who has viewed them. So, what I'm getting at is, if you just view a man's profile, it's very likely he's going to know it. In fact it's probably part of his routine when he logs in. Well, guess what? That's all you have to do. It's not being the

aggressor. It's more like you showed up at the same bar as he did, and now you're going to find out if he likes what he sees and approaches you, or if he's making a beeline for what's-her-face. I don't know about you, but I want the man who's making the beeline for me.

But what if he sees that I viewed him and didn't send him a message or flirt? Won't he think I'm not interested, even if I am?

Possibly, but if that it stops him from contacting you, you don't want him anyway. Men who like what they see, and have some balls, will respond to you and say something like, "I noticed you dropped by…" or "thanks for dropping by, I like your profile, would you like to chat?" Bottom line is, if he doesn't respond to you after you viewed him, there are only two possibilities (1) something about your profile didn't work for him, or (2) if he liked your profile but chose not to respond because you didn't send him a flirt, he's got some kind of serious holier-than-thou attitude you don't need to be dealing with, girlfriend. Move on!

Still having a hard time with this one? Here's another way of thinking about it if the bar scene scenario didn't sell you.

> • When you do a search, you have specific, basic, criteria that you use – distance, whether or not he has a photo posted, height, weight, age range, and so forth. You use this basic search

criteria to generate a list of men whom you then review, starting with their photo. If you like the photo, you click on it to find out more about him. If you like him, you (well you won't anymore, but have in the past) send him an email or flirt.

- Now, let's not think about you, let's think about him. He does everything you did, only, at the end of the story, he doesn't send you an email or a flirt. Girlfriend, you need to see the writing on the wall. He came, he saw, and he kept going. It's not that bad. Indeed, it frees up your time for the men who stopped dead in their tracks blown away by everything you have to offer. These are the men who will contact you.

Still not happy with the idea of having to sit back and wait for the man to approach? Let's take this down to the bare bones. It might be about needing to be in control. Putting your profile on more than one website multiplies your chances of men noticing you. Think of it this way - you are in control when you respond only to the men who are interested in you. If you're out there sending flirts and messages to everyone who looks half decent, hoping he will respond, that is out of control. You and I both know you're better than that.

But I just know my Mr. Perfect is looking for me, Diane, and I'm worried if I do this your way, he will never find me!

This is your excuse for why you need to go and find him, right? Wrong.

- If you meet his search criteria, he will find you.

- If you don't meet his search criteria, then he's not your Mr. Perfect. Get it?

But I keep getting emails and flirts from total losers who aren't attractive and totally not my type.

This is perfect, and it's a great segue into my next spiel.

The ~~two~~ three-point disability:

Do you know your number? Come on now, you know what I'm talking about – the scale of 1 to 10. Are you a 2, a 7 or a Bo Derek 10? Be realistic about this. You really need to know your number, because if you do, this will all make sense. Let's say, for now, you're a 7.

Men, the poor creatures, seem to have a disability they are unaware of. It's called the 2-point disability. What does it mean? It means that if they are a 5, they will think they are a 7. If they are an 8, they will think they are a 10.

Now take that disability and apply it to dating (Internet or otherwise). Suddenly it grows. Now, all at once, the 2-point disability becomes 3. What I mean is, men who are 5s will, without even thinking twice, start with women who are

8s. Start there. Why? Well, I suspect it has to do with rejection. It's much easier to have your flirt ignored than have a drink thrown in your face. No doubt there's also a whole pile of psychology behind it that is connected to his relationship with his mother, yadda, yadda, yadda, but right now, who cares? We're in real-time here. You've got men sending you emails and flirts while you are reading this book, and you need answers.

So, remember I said above that you're a 7. Remember you said above, *"But I keep getting emails and flirts from total losers who aren't attractive and totally not my type."* There you go. There's your answer to why this is happening. You're getting hint on by 4s and the odd 5. Men have a tendency to overrate themselves and therefore, shop beyond their budget. They are hoping (and some are expecting) to find the steal of the century, and will go to as many window displays as they have to in order to get it.

My advice on this one? Don't sweat it. Just keep viewing men you like and deleting those you don't until you come across someone you think you could stand to look at long enough to share a cup of coffee or a meal. It's really that simple.

I don't want to sound like your mother, but I've totally learned that looks aren't everything. One of the best lovers I ever had wasn't what I would call traditionally good looking (aka Brad Pitt), but he was super charismatic in person, extremely smart, and managed to fill every room he walked into. Once I met him and spent a little time with him, I found a whole bunch about him that I liked, and not one of them had to do with his facial features. Turned out he was hung like a horse as well. Not bad! So, what's the moral here? No need to explain, I think you get it.

Realistically, we all know the only way a guy who (in real life) is actually a 5 or a 6, can get a girl who's a 9 or above, is if he happens to have a shit load of money. They'll try though, Lord knows they'll try.

Standards – Set 'em and Stick to 'em:

Whatever you do, you will never let your standards drop. What do I mean? Standards – the opposite is the "At least he's…"

Let me clarify:

- *At least he's* not holding his dick underneath his clothing like that other guy was.

I'm warning you now, if you don't have standards, this thinking will eventually happen!

- *At least he* didn't take a photo of himself in the bathroom mirror with a cell phone. Groan.

- *At least he's* honest about being married. There are so many substandard guys out there that married men who are looking for some booty on the side are starting to look good?

Yeah, sure, laugh about it all you want. The reality is, after a couple months of Internet dating, maybe fewer, you'll be ready to pull your hair out (this is where that wig comes in handy), and that's the exact moment when you're most vulnerable to falling prey to the "at least he's."

So what's a standard?

We are going to see our standards in action as we wade through the next chapter, but basically you are setting your standards by knowing exactly what you are looking for. That includes making up your mind, once and for all, about the kind of relationship you want.

First, what kind of guy do you want? In my interpretation, there are three basic categories of men:

1.   Mr. Right for One Night:

I don't make rules. I completely understand the need to "get jiggy with it" once in a while. I mean, it's okay to settle for less, so long as you only settle for it for one night. More on that later.

2.   Borderline Boy:

This is the guy who manages to slide under the wire. He's never really good enough, but when you compare him to some of the others you met (online or otherwise), he seems to shine like a star. This is the most troublesome type. He has the potential to suck up all your time and emotional energy (not to mention money) and keep you from moving on. If you're with a Borderline Boy, you already know it. Look at the calendar. Has it been more than two years?

Yes. Look at your left hand. No ring, right? Of course not.

Damn it, Diane, you're right.

I know, let's move on.

3.   A Penis with Potential:

The penis is sufficient, and it works. The man attached to it ain't half bad either. All right, we're finally making progress.

Did I just hear you say you want a Penis with Potential?

Congratulations! You now know what you won't settle for, and that includes any guy whose profile suggests he's Mr. Right For One Night or has the potential to become a Borderline Boy.

So, before we move on to Chapter 3 (and this is going to be some kind of fun), let's agree as follows.

Diane, I am looking for a real relationship. Therefore, I promise I will not:

☐ Forget the Caveman Rules and your silly princess stories.

☐ Whine that life isn't fair.

☐ Do anything more than post my profile, view some men, then sit back and wait for my inbox to fill up.

☐ Forget your numbers disability theory.

☐ Fall prey to the **"At least he's…"**

☐ Put a profile on the same website twice, tsk, tsk.

☐ Forget that what I want more than anything is a Penis with Potential.

Your autograph please:

_____

You have to have standards, because if you don't, you won't be able to wade through the shit successfully. On that topic, let's keep clickin'.

CHAPTER 3

WADING THROUGH THE SHIT

You already know finding your Mr. Right (not Mr. Right Now, or Mr. Right For One Night) isn't going to be easy.

Remember when I referred to "the substandard" in the introduction? Well, now you're actually going to meet them and delete them.

Caveman rules, he pursues, you respond. So when you log into the website, you're going straight to the inbox.

The first step, before opening any messages, is to remind yourself of your standards. Don't fall into the "At least he's…" trap.

Up for Immediate Deletion:

I don't know what the hell is going on in some men's minds when they create their profiles. Well, then again, maybe I do. As Patti Stanger (Millionaire Matchmaker) always says, "The penis does the picking." It not only does the picking, but in the case of these guys, it's doing the thinking too. Remember how you used to believe "Men think with their small heads" was a joke? Check out these dudes. Oh, and because you have standards, you will absolutely not respond to:

- <u>Thick11</u> – Let me guess. He's referring to his dick? Delete.
- <u>BigWilly7</u> – Let me guess, he's referring to his dick, and didn't realize that his competition is 4 inches bigger. Delete.
- <u>OneWang</u> – Do you know anyone that has two? Let's face it. Wang computers have been gone for eons so there's no way this dude isn't violating the "don't refer to your damn dick" rule. Delete.
- <u>TotalFreedom</u> – If this is what he's looking for, it's not exactly what commitment-minded women should waste her time on. Delete.
- <u>Juicy69Babe</u> - Seriously, how many men are actually good at this? Besides, isn't a "babe" usually a woman? This one is all wrong. Delete.
- <u>Jean11Hot</u> – Are these guys ever hot? No. End of discussion. Delete.

- <u>BootyDaddy07</u> – There's just something creepy about a guy who calls himself "Daddy." The only possible thing that could make this even remotely okay was if he was a multi-gazillionaire, but he's not. Delete.

- <u>BigBaller727</u> – Unless this guy is a pro baseball player, this is simply too much information. Delete.

- <u>FonzyHot</u> – Okay this isn't the worst I've ever seen, but let's think about this. Was Fonzy actually hot? If you think he was, then fine. Otherwise – Delete.

Not all sites are the same, but if you can spot these names in your inbox and delete them without even reading the message or the flirt, perfect. Unless, of course, you're curious to see what Thick11 actually looks like…

Do respond to these guys, **but only if they meet your standards**. They are at least making an effort. These are my initial reactions to their profile names:

- <u>CoolSugaCane</u> – Hints at his heritage and makes me think we'll have a fun, relaxed first date.

- <u>Don1959</u> – Normal. Hi, my name is Don and I was born in 1959. Good.

- <u>SpecialKFun</u> – I'm expecting two things, (1) his name starts with the letter "K" and, (2) that our first date will be at a comedy club. Even if that isn't the case, it's a positive first impression to make.

- <u>Kinglookg4Queen</u> – I like it. At least he's upfront about wanting a woman in his life. Unless some other part of his profile is a disaster, this is a promising start.

- <u>MauiBoy</u> – He's been there, lives there or wants to go there, it's all good.

Bookmarks, brides and other profile disasters:

After you weed out the bad profile names, I strongly suggest you save yourself some headaches and delete the following as well, no matter how cute you think he is:

- <u>3 or 4 kids, never married, lives in Georgia, Texas (or anywhere else that requires him to travel to get to you)</u> - Okay there are a couple of problems here, but let's face it, the biggest one is that no matter how much money he makes, after he's paid child support for all those kids, he won't be getting on no plane. This guy needs to date someone on his street. The fact that he's had all these kids without marrying the baby-mama(s) – strike 2. You find out he's not paying child support – strike 10! Run for the hills!

- <u>Jesus wallpaper</u> – If you're Christian and want to hang with a Christian, it might be cool, but be weary of the troller who is simply doing it to add some Christian-booty notches to his bedpost.

- <u>God-fearing</u> – Unless the words God-fearing strikes a chord deep within your soul, I'd recommend steering away from those who feel compelled to profess this. I always wonder why these folks aren't on some of the more specific sites like ChristianMingle.com. Wouldn't it be easier to meet someone with same beliefs in a forum like that?

- <u>40-year-old student</u> – Okay, my friend, let's not support a man through his mid-life crisis. It was cool the first time, back when you were both in college. Now, I'm sorry to say, it's just plain desperate. Any man over the age of 40 who hasn't settled on a career isn't about to settle on a woman, not the way you want him to anyway.

- <u>Legally separated</u> – Can you say unfinished business? Unless you're a sucker for punishment and want to be dragged through all the drama of a messy divorce, only to find out you're the transition girl, I'd stay far away from this one. Legally separated is also a handy category for married men who claim to be sleeping on the couch. No matter how you slice it, it just isn't good.

- <u>Men who post photos of themselves handling their dicks, or showing outlines of erections under clothing</u> – Oh man, where do I start? The fundamental problem is that he thinks this is a good idea. *What he thinks*, get it? Clearly this is all he has to offer, which is why he's made it a point of emphasis. If this is what he thinks, then trust me when I say, it's true (you are what you believe, yadda, yadda, yadda). Don't go looking for a nice car, good job, and supportive friend if you meet this Dick for coffee.

- <u>Smokers</u> – One week on the patch does not a "non-smoker" make. Keep your nose open for the telltale signs and remember how difficult it really is to kick this habit.

- <u>Any man who takes photos of himself in the bathroom mirror (typically with a cell phone)</u> – Why is this happening you ask? And if you're not asking, you should be. The answer is simple. He has no friends. No friends, no family, no sister, no cousin, nobody at all who could possibly invest two minutes of their time to take a photo of him. Why? Need I say more?

- <u>Guys who post photos of everything they own</u> – Is this a dating website, or are we posting inventory for insurance purposes? He just sent me a flirt that said, "Smile." Why do I need to see his dining room table? Do I care? Am I assessing his personal net worth based on a recent sale at Macy's? Something is wrong here. It's making me think of the Dick dilemma, like maybe he doesn't think he's good enough, so he's letting me know he comes with a dowry. But wait. Isn't that supposed to be the woman, and isn't it like a goat or something?

- <u>Guys who post photos of under-age children</u> – This is just wrong, wrong, wrong! Even though the thinking behind it is probably, love me, love my kids, to me it shows a blatant lack of respect for his children's safety and privacy, not to mention a lack of common sense. Children should be integrated into relationships slowly, over time. Delete this baby-daddy wants a babysitter immediately. You are not a nanny.

- <u>Looking for a pen pal</u> – Also known as, "looking for smut talk on MSN messenger while my wife or girlfriend is out of the house." Not even remotely good enough. If you have time on your hands and want to spend it fulfilling some creep's fantasy, go ahead, make his day. Okay, okay, so this particular guy is not a total creep. Still he is on a dating website saying that he's looking for a pen pal. Why? Don't waste your time figuring it out. You have serious men to reply to.

- <u>No photo</u> – He's either married or so ugly you're not going to want to see the photo anyway. Don't waste your time. He's probably not wasting his time sending messages to girls without photos. After all, he contacted you, right?

- <u>Oh my God, did he crop out the bride?</u> – I've seen this, I actually have! The veil on his left shoulder, the train of her dress behind his feet. Is this the last time he was cleaned up and in a suit? What are these men thinking? I know what I'm thinking and it starts with "d," delete.

- <u>Bookmarks</u> – Some dating sites have what they call bookmarks. They let you know the man has viewed your profile and bookmarked you. For what? A later date? Until he decides he can't find anyone better? A man who sends you a bookmark is no different than a man who shows up for dinner with no wine. I don't think so! Not only is it rude, he may as well be saying, *I'll get around to you when I have time.*

A bookmark is not a sign of a nice, timid, introverted man who is simply misunderstood. No. A bookmark is a bookmark. You put it in your book because you want to remember where you left off. Don't respond to a man who was scrolling through pages of woman and bookmarked you because he wants to remember where he left off.

Say What? A Whole New Use of the English Language:

These lovely little tidbits were taken off real life profiles:

"The three things you are most thankful for: *I am thankful for my 3 dotters.*"

Okay, tell me something, is this guy playing bingo or is he referring to his kids?

"I have 3 daughters who live with me. I devote my life and all my time to them. I am 39 and 100% single and dramma free. Right now in my life I don't need a women. Shareing the world with the 3 that I have makes my world perfect."

Then what the hell is he doing on a dating site? This is bizarre to me! Also, "Drama" and "sharing" could use a little help Remember, spell check, spell check, spell check.

"If you love candle light dinners, flowers for no reason, than I'm your MAN. Also just to hear those three WORDS anytime as we mature into soul mate than I'm your MAN. But mostly yearning and anticipation of giving hot bubble baths with tantalizing foot massages as we endure cuddling, conversations as we fall to sleep!!!!! Than I'm your MAN!"

I'm confused, but at least I know his plan is to be, MY MAN! Let's get out a thesaurus and look up ENDURE. Nope, just as I thought, it's not good. People endure hunger and torture, not cuddling. Duh!

> **DIANE SAYS:** Be wary of the guy who claims he doesn't post a photo due to a high profile job, because he's FBI, a cop, or any other "high security" reason. If you really and truly have a position that requires that much discretion, why choose Internet dating to begin with? There are plenty of traditional methods these folks can access. My point is, I really don't think there is such a thing as a good reason to not post a photo, unless, of course, you're married, or in a relationship, hummm...

A few other points to consider when reviewing his profile:

☐   An un-tucked shirt and double-chin are telltale signs he hasn't been "athletic" since high school.

☐   If the smile doesn't show his teeth, there's a good chance something is wrong with them.

☐   If a guy won't show you his boobs, then you know he has them. Be aware of head shots or photos cropped off just above the *mansiere.*

If weight, teeth, and (lack of) man-boobs are important to you, I strongly suggest you ask him to send you more photos. If he won't, you have your answer. If he has a million excuses as to why he doesn't have more photos, you still have your answer.

Now, because we're at the end of this chapter, you had to know this is coming next.

Diane, I am looking for a real relationship. Therefore, I promise I will not:

☐ Ever, ever, respond to Thick11 or BigWilly7. I understand what you mean when you say they are not Penises with Potential.

☐ Delete SpecialKFun if he meets all my standards, even though he is a 5 and I am a 7. I will at least make an effort to have a coffee with him.

☐ Seriously consider any of the men who you identified in this chapter, unless I am only looking for a Mr. Right For One Night.

Your autograph please:

_____

Congratulations. You've successfully waded through more shit than you ever imagined possible, and have come out smelling like a rose. Now that the junk is out of your trunk, let's talk about connecting. Grab your mouse, and let's keep clickin'.

CHAPTER 4

NOW THAT THE JUNK IS OUT OF YOUR TRUNK

Hello! **The word is respond, not bond:**
Respond. Defined by Merriam-Webster as *to act in response* or, *to show favorable reaction.*

The word does not mean chase. Caveman rules. We do not chase men; we respond to men. Translated to the internet, it means we hit reply, not send. Keep this in mind.

All right, you've cleared your inbox of all potential disasters and are ready for the next step. Great. When it comes to responding, there are three distinct parts:

- Assessing
- Timing
- Composing

Assessing:

What are you going to assess first and foremost? Come on, this is a skill-testing question, girlfriend. What?

I know, Diane! I'm going to determine if he meets my standards.

Right.

So before we worry about how long we should wait to respond, let's see if he's even worth your time. Open up the message and check out his profile.

Done? Okay, let's assume he appears normal. He didn't call himself BootyDaddy07, he didn't post pictures of his kids, and he lives within a reasonable commuting distance (not to mention everything else on your list). Next, let's see what the message says.

I think this part is pretty straightforward, but just in case it's not, here are some real examples of things men have said in their first message to me.

You will delete:

- "You are very sexy. I want you in my bed."

Try not to be flattered by this. This man has no class. He either isn't looking for a real relationship (despite what his profile says), or he has yet to learn that if he's truly interested in a woman, he should approach her in a classy way. Either way, it's not good.

- "I love toes. Please let me suck your toes. I have a foot fetish, and I love women's toes, all kinds of toes."

I'm thinking I don't need to explain this one. No matter how hot he might be, don't even go there. Your toes and only your toes will never be enough for this guy. I don't know about you, but the last thing I ever want to tell my friends and family is, "I caught him in bed, sucking another woman's toes."

- "I thought you'd like me. I guess u don't like me."

This is a note I received from a man after viewing his profile (remember Who Viewed Me, in Chapter 4?) A woman's immediate reaction might be to feel sorry for him and respond right away. I'm betting he knows that, and it's worked for him in the past. Not with you, my friend. Not with you.

You wouldn't be caught dead saying: "Oh no, that's not the case at all, I did like you. That's why I was looking at your profile." No, no, no.

Why? Because this man hasn't even connected with you electronically, and he is defeated already. He's either trying to manipulate you, or he's assuming you didn't like him (a very clear indicator of low self-esteem). Remember what they taught you in school about the word *assume*? It makes an **ass** out of **u** and **me**. You don't have time for this. The only time the word ass should come up in this whole process is when he meets you, sees yours, and is crazy about how good it looks.

You will respond to:

> • Hello. I came across your profile, and I live close to you. I'd be very interested in getting to know more about you. You're a very attractive woman.

> • Hey, I am John. What's your name?

> • Hi, I'm Ricardo. I liked your profile. I'd like to take you for coffee, or dancing, whatever you like.

All right, now that you have weeded through a hundred emails and found one man who appears to meet your standards, let's talk about timing.

Timing:

Let me start by saying I am not a fan of the hard-fast rule of purposely waiting 48 hours to respond to a man. Why would you? Just because you want to appear busy? No. What you're really going to appear, in today's world, is disconnected.

How many people do you know who have a cell phone, iPhone or Blackberry? Everyone does now, whether they're eight or eighty, and we get our messages from everywhere, no matter where we are. For example, if you post a message on your friend's Facebook wall, chances are they got it instantly via their phone. So, pretending you don't realize you have a message really is that, pretending.

This isn't about playing games, it's about finding love. Besides, how quickly you respond is a hundred times more important *after* you've established a dating relationship than it is when you haven't even met for coffee.

My only rules in the timing department are:

      1. Don't respond immediately

      2. Don't respond on Friday or Saturday nights after 4:00 p.m.

For example: You're online surfing men and viewing their profiles when one of them happens to send you a message. First and foremost, remember your standards! Check out his profile thoroughly. Then, if he makes the cut, leave his message in your inbox and continue to surf.

Later, if you feel compelled, respond to him just before you sign off for the night. If it's Friday or Saturday night, wait until after 10:00 a.m. the next morning.

DIANE SAYS: Do not engage in any instant messaging (IM) sessions. Never. It doesn't matter how boring your night is. More on this, later in the chapter.

Composing:

You just have to know that I'm going to give you another template, right? It's easy. No matter what he said in his initial contact, your first reply will always be these three simple sentences:

Hi, my name is <first name only>. Thank you for your message. I like your profile.

That's it. Easy peasy. Just as we discussed before, don't waffle on. Keep it simple and to the point. Why the brief reply? Well, not only because it's a tad psycho to tell him about all your hopes, dreams, and relationship expectations when you haven't even met him, but also because, you want to see what he does next. If you've been dating online, you know what can happen. Men who appear to meet your standards can pull you down into the gutter of smut talk in a heartbeat.

What you're looking for is consistency. Meaning, you want to see him demonstrate that he is a gentleman, consistently. If he can't do it in writing, I guarantee he can't do in person. What you're also looking for is a reasonable desire to (a) connect by phone, and then, (b) meet in person. A total of four to five emails are enough:

1.   He sends his initial contact email (or the flirt, smile, or wink).

2.   You send the brief reply.

3.   He responds.

4.   You send a brief reply.

5.   He responds and attempts to initiate a phone conversation.

6.   You respond positively.

Easy enough? I thought so.

Backing up a bit here, you may be wondering what I meant by *a reasonable desire* to call or connect. What I mean is, not tonight, not tomorrow, but also, not after months of emailing to and fro. Some of this will depend on distance, jobs, or children. However, my advice to you is to get him on the phone as soon as it's convenient. Phone conversations can tell you a lot about a man. Always listen and pay attention to things like:

- The guy who calls you from a bar, or on the street, or anywhere that is loud, noisy, and distracting.

- The guy who calls you from home with the TV on in the background, his attention waning in and out as his team gets close to the goal.

- The guy who calls from home, at a good time, but proceeds to tell you his first ex-wife took everything he had, and his second ex-wife tried to poison him. Yes, yes, this really happened, groan.

- The guy who is so hungry he absolutely has to eat while he's on the phone with you.

- The guy who always calls you from his car.

I find that people really tell you who they are when you not only listen to them, but when you also pay attention to *their* surroundings. The guy you want to meet for coffee will have the decency and consideration to call when he is in a quiet place, can focus on the conversation, isn't distracted by the game, isn't hungry, and isn't escaping heaven knows what at home to call you from his car.

Now, what to do about those flirts, smiles, and winks? Basically you start in the same place—making sure he meets the standards. Repeat:

Hi, my name is <first name only>. Thank you for the <flirt, smile, whatever>. I like your profile.

What you have to remember about this guy is that it's highly unlikely he's read your profile the first time around. Now that he's gotten a reply from you, he should. Pay attention as to whether or not he addresses something you said about yourself, and I don't mean the basic tombstone stuff like city, eye color, height, and weight. I mean the *About Me* section. If you mentioned you had a dog, what you're looking for him to say is something like: "I have a dog too, his name is Buckley, and he's a black lab."

What if you've had more than six email exchanges, all of which have been tasteful, and yet he hasn't initiated a phone conversation? Simple. Stop corresponding with him. If you don't get a follow-up email from him in the next couple of days suggesting a call, move on. SPECIALKFUN isn't busy and he knows how to dial a phone. You're not looking for email buddies here, you're looking for love.

- *What if he's busy?*

He's not. How could he be too busy to call you but not too busy to email you?

- *What if he's shy?*

He's not. He's posted his picture on the internet for the entire world to see.

• *What if he doesn't have a long-distance calling plan?*

He should. If he's initiating contact with women that far away, he better hurry up and get one. Even the gas station sells calling cards.

• *What if he's inundated with flirts, smiles, winks, and emails from all those other women who haven't read this book?*

He is. And that's not good enough for you. You deserve a man who doesn't suffer from OADD, Online Attention Deficit Disorder. You deserve a man who can focus on you long enough to initiate a phone call.

Get my point?

Good. Let's move on

Romancing the Stone—Ignore the non-responders:

It doesn't matter how many email exchanges you had, how good they were, or how many times you fantasized about your wedding. If it seems to be going along well, then suddenly he doesn't respond to your email, don't email him! That is chasing, and we don't chase; we respond. Remember?

Don't wait a week then send him a note asking him how he's doing. Don't wait two weeks then send him a note asking him if everything is all right because you are worried. Don't wait three weeks then send him a note telling him he's an asshole for ditching out on you. Just don't. **Men who disappear are not:**

- lying in a ditch, dying, in desperate need of your help;

- on a plane to Haiti to save orphaned children; or,

- suffering from a computer crash which caused him to lose everyone's email address, including yours.

They are out on a date with someone else, and by now, you should be too.

If three months later, Mr. MAUIBOY dares to show up in your inbox again, what will you do? Delete. You're not interested in reading his tale of woe. You're also not interested in reading an email that comes across like nothing is wrong. Just delete him.

Moral of the story: You don't have time to waste on non-responders. With over 50 million people online, at least half of which are men, you've got 25 million other guys with more promise than him.

Sorry, MAUIBOY, you're not a Penis With Potential.

Romancing the Bone—Avoid the smut-talkers:

Let me start by saying it's not rude to ignore an Instant Message, even if your site has the feature that shows *Who's Online*. You can blame it on your cat who stepped on your keyboard, your pop-up blocker, or the fact that you had so many men IM-ing you that you couldn't answer them all, and definitely didn't see his. The reality is, you don't engage this way. Trust me when I say I've fallen prey to it on many occasions, mostly out of curiosity, and nine times out of ten, the guy either:

(a) started to get sexually suggestive within minutes;

(b) typed so slow I lost my patience; or,

(c) was clearly carrying on multiple IM conversations, so much so that a couple of the answers to my questions didn't make sense.

It's not the way to go.

Diane, I am looking for a real relationship. Therefore, I promise I will not:

☐   Chase a man. It violates the caveman rules.

☐   Respond to self-professed fetish-ites, who appear to like my feet, shoes, ear lobes, or anything else in my pictures better than he likes me.

☐   Console a man who feels rejected, especially when I haven't even met him.

☐   Respond immediately.

☐   Engage in smut, or any other kind of talk via instant messaging sessions.

☐   SEND EMAILS, IN CAPITAL LETTERS, TO MEN WHO ARE TOO FUCKING RUDE TO REPLY TO MY EMAILS!

Your autograph please:

_____

All right, the easy part is over. Now you actually have to meet him in person. Take a big, deep breath and let's keep clickin'.

CHAPTER 5

<u>FART BOY AND OTHER FIRST-DATE BOMBS</u>

Two Dates in One—The first and the last:

It's hard to believe but true. This man traveled a couple of hours to meet me. I lived on an island at the time, so a ferry ride was involved to get there. He said he ran his own company but was also into herbal products. Even went so far as to claim that nobody could tell how old he was because of them. I know a sales pitch when I hear one, so I politely answered in a neutral way without showing any interest in looking younger myself. When he arrived, I recognized him from his photos, but my first impression was, yes, I'd guess he was in his early forties. So much for the herbs.

We spent a few hours together and ended up going for dinner. He had a few quirks, but I'll focus on the main event. After dinner we were walking back to my place when he decided to hold my hand. Okay, it's not the end of the world. I wasn't totally feeling the guy, but up to that point, I didn't feel like running away either. He was talking when suddenly I heard him fart. I couldn't believe it and I thought I was mistaken. He just kept talking and walking, still holding my hand, when it happened again, and I don't mean a little puffer fart. I mean the big roller coaster kind. The kind you can't miss, the kind that if he was sitting, would have made him lean to the left. I was in shock, and my immediate reaction was to drop my purse. That way I could let go of his hand to gather my things off the ground. When I stood back up, needless to say, the purse was in the hand between us. I was traumatized. It was the grossest thing I'd ever experienced on a date. Ever.

The odd thing was there was no reaction from him. He kept talking and walking as if nothing had happened. No excuses, no apologies, nothing. To him, this was normal and I realized he was covertly telling me, "You better be okay with this." Well, guess what? I wasn't.

The rest of the way home, I couldn't think of anything else. I was grossed out and could barely engage in conversation anymore. *This*, I thought to myself, *was his first-date behavior? Just imagine what it will be like a couple of years from now when he's comfortable.* Will he just fart and belch out loud in the restaurant? What about planes? Cars? With friends and family around? It was simply disgusting behavior to me and a very clear indication of what the future with him would be like. I couldn't get him back to the ferry fast enough.

The interesting part is how this story ends. A few days later, he sent me a note. All it said was, "Was I really that disgusting?"

I don't know about you, but my first thought was, if you have to ask, you already know the answer. I didn't respond. He did not meet my standards; he was not a PWP. I simply hit delete.

Getting back to you.

You walk into the coffee shop at exactly 7:05 pm, and there he is. Instantly you know he's not the one for you. It's something about the way he looks when he smiles. It's just not the same in person. Damn it. He stands and reaches out to shake your hand, and you look away. Shit. Now what?

Well, for one, let's make sure you're following your head, not your crotch. Maybe there wasn't an immediate stirring in the loins, but that doesn't necessarily mean he won't be good in bed.

Good point, Diane.

I know.

Force yourself to stay and get through the coffee date at least. You may discover something about him that intrigues you. Maybe he has a much better personality than you expected. Maybe he's a really good listener. Maybe he has a really big dick.

I'm just kidding.

No you're not, Diane.

Damn. You're right, I'm not. Anyway, my point is, whatever he has that might end up changing your mind about him may take a little while to discover.

It's not working. He didn't offer to buy coffee, he snorts like a pig when he laughs, and he has a problem making eye contact. To top it all off, he launched into the story of his life, and in less than twenty minutes, you discovered that he (a) doesn't know who is father is, (b) is aware of some big family secret about who the man might actually be, (c) is a member of CODA, a support organization for people who are co-dependent, (d) has particularly strong political views that are opposite to yours, and (e) has a job that requires him to work nights and weekends.

This simply won't do, and that's okay. It's a perfect example of two dates in one. You met him, listened to him, and made the assessment that he didn't meet your standards. Not one of them. As a result, you ended the date politely and went home. **What you did not do is** turn into Cinderella's sister and try to fit a foot that was too big into a tiny glass slipper. You are not desperate for a man, any man. You didn't choose to think, "Poor him. How can I help him find his real father?" You also didn't chose to ignore the fact that he self-professed his membership in CODA. Good.

Nobody's perfect, Diane.

I know. I'm not judging the man. I'm celebrating your decision to make sure the one you end up with meets your standards. Now, let's take a closer look at some very important warning signs.

Spot the defects and return the goods:

Defects. Major ones. The run-for-the-hills kind. The kind that will impact you for the rest of your life if you end up with this guy. You know what I mean. Alcohol, anger, sexual addictions. The signs may be difficult to spot in the first few dates, but not impossible. Trends always develop. The key is to listen, observe, make note of the clues, and, most important, don't choose to ignore them. When it's raining red flags, there's a reason, my friend.

How do you spot the problems? It may take a couple of dates, but I've been on enough to know there are some early warning signs you must clue into. Read on.

Is that really his tenth beer? Alcoholic:

You won't have to hang with this guy long before the signs will surface, and believe it or not, there usually enough hints in the first three dates to make a reasonable judgment call. Just pay attention, and don't make excuses for him. What do I mean by that? Don't fall for any of these. They are all clues and should be put on your list:

○ "I need it to unwind," or, "It helps me unwind."

▪ The problem words here are "need" and "help." You can unwind without it. Why can't he?

○ I need a drink. My _____ (boss, ex-girlfriend, best friend) was such a _____ (asshole, bitch, jerk) to me today, I can't believe it.

▪ Blaming someone else for why he has to drink.

○ Sorry, I tend to drink a lot when I'm nervous.

▪ If he's just nervous, one drink and an hour with you should be enough to calm him down. There's no need to empty a bottle.

If, during your first three dates, you go out for dinner, you also need to watch for these two, very important clues:

1. How fast he drinks. Does he make a glass of wine look like a shooter?

2. What does he want to do next? If he has three drinks or more, pay attention to what he wants to do after dinner. Does it have to include alcohol, or is he happy with going to a movie? Once

the booze gets flowing, these guys don't want to stop.

Watch for the early warning signs, take note of them, and take them seriously. You want a man who's in love with you, not a bottle. If you hang with this guy, his addiction will become your relationships' biggest problem. Unless you're looking for something new to spend $150.00 an hour talking to your shrink about, get out of it! Pick up your purse, and move on.

Was it really that bad? Anger:

Impatience often precedes anger. Pay close attention to a man who gets jumpy just waiting in line to buy a coffee. This isn't something you want to mess around with. You're going to really need to watch this one closely if during the first couple of dates, he does any of the following:

o He yells, shouts, screams, or swears at anyone while he's driving.

o He talks about people (friends, family, co-workers) and the grudges he's still holding against them.

o He is unreasonably confrontational or angry about something you say or do during the date.

o He appears impatient, especially when you ask him a lot of questions, or if it's his turn to listen to you for any length of time.

       ○ You get the sense that he may be moody, or you have seen evidence of it already.

You notice one of these? Make a note. You notice two of them? Make two notes and stick 'em on your forehead so you don't forget them. You notice three? Dump this guy's ass! You don't want to be his next grudge. Or worse yet, punching bag. If you eventually fall in love with him, you'll end up living with a ticking time bomb, and you'll never know when it'll go off. This is one area where you *must* follow your instincts, you *must* gather the clues, and you *must* take action. Don't even think about it. Pick up your purse and move on.

He can only do it how? Sexual obsession/addiction:

If you're not comfortable with it, don't do it. If it's not legal, don't do it. If you think it will go away if only he had "the love of the right woman" (and that woman, of course, is you), you're wrong. If at any time during your initial conversations, or first three dates, he confides any of the following or demonstrates any of the following behavior, put it on your list:

       ○ He can't get turned on unless you're willing to dress up in sex-related costumes, and I mean, every single time.

       ○ He frequents strip clubs, topless bars, or other sex-related facilities *alone*.

       ○ He says that he needs sex more than once a day.

o He flirts with other women while he's with you or stares at women's butts, boobs, or other body parts, and doesn't care if you notice.

o He makes sexual comments about other people to you or is sexually inappropriate during dinner.

If you fall in love with a sex addict, you'll be cheating yourself out of happiness, and he'll be cheating because he'll never be satisfied. Grab your nurse's costume, shove it in your bag, and get out of there. You don't need the itchy-scratchies or bill from the doctor that'll go along with it.

<u>His boss did it to him again. Victim</u>:

Everyone is always out to get a victim. It doesn't matter if it's the cashier at the grocery store who didn't give him the correct amount of change or the grade eight teacher who gave him a C when he deserved an A. Ooh, and let me point out that the older the stories are, the longer he's lived with his victim mentality, and therefore, the harder it will be to change. Listen, listen, listen, to what he's telling you. Victims love their victim-ness, and it's rare for them to get through one date (let alone three) without diving into a Poor Me story.

Easy-to-spot-on-a-date victim behaviors:

o He may be very disinterested in listening to what you have to say and very interested in talking about himself.

o His stories are likely to be riddled with a lot of complaining and blaming of others.

o He may try to make you feel guilty. Perhaps when the bill arrives, he'll say jokingly, "Wow, I'm going to have to work overtime for a week to pay for this."

o His conversation will include a lot of phrases like, "I won't," "I can't," "I'll never."

You, my friend, are going to gather these clues and realize it's not your job to fix him. A skilled professional would be challenged to correct this pattern of thinking. If you fall in love with a victim, you'll just end up being the next person whose fault everything is. You don't need any new projects. Your only project is you, and you want love. Pick up your purse and go home.

He said they're just friends. Past Relationship Recovery:

He doesn't think he's easy to spot, but he is. This guy:

o Sets up dates in obscure locations.

▪ He doesn't want anyone he knows to see him with you. They might report back to *her*.

o Has difficulty being, or refuses to be, physically affectionate with you in public.

- He doesn't want anyone he knows to see him with you, and if they do, he wants to be able to say you're "just friends." It means he still has feelings for *her*, and he doesn't want to spoil it in case she is thinking about coming back.

o Talks about her or continues to communicate with her.

- A man who is over a chick doesn't talk about her or continue to talk to her. If he makes a point of telling you about her and how they are still friends, it doesn't mean he's a nice guy. It means he's not over her.

o Won't open up.

- He appears to have difficulty showing emotions, especially the positive ones like happiness, excitement, and desire. After all, he's still suffering because of his feelings for *her*.

o Cries on your shoulder about how terrible his relationship with his ex was, and all the things she did wrong.

You don't want someone who is still pining for *her*. You want someone who's crazy about you. If you fall in love with this guy, you'll be sleeping on your phone waiting for it to ring.

The problem is, it won't. Recovery counselor, you are not and last you checked the Coach bag you just bought wasn't white, and it didn't have a red cross on the side. Girlfriend, pick up your purse and move on.

<u>It's my way or the highway. Control Freak</u>:

This guy might seem like he's "being the man," but he's probably not. He needs to make all the decisions himself. He will do some or all of the following:

○ Ensure the first and all dates and locations fit *his* schedule.

○ Insist on driving, paying the bill, and planning what happens next.

○ Be compulsive about something such as how the food is cooked or arranged on his plate or how many times he washes his hands. He may check all the cutlery for cleanliness before using it.

○ Order your food or tell you what you should/should not have.

○ He won't share anything, not an appetizer, not a piece of his steak.

○ He may compliment you, but then later say something like, "You should wear your hair short. I think it would look great that way."

We all have a little freak in us somewhere, but Sleeping With the Enemy just isn't cool. You know what to do. Reach down, pick it up, and move on.

<u>All he needs is love. Childhood emotional damage</u>:

And you're just the woman to give it to him? No. No, you certainly are not. Depending on the kind of childhood abuse (sexual, physical, abandonment, religious fanaticism) this relationship may never get off the ground. If he identifies his issue, but, again, fails to identify what he's done to recover from it, you should count the clues, do some research, and make a decision about him with your head, not your heart.

Signs you need to watch for, generally, include any disproportionate amount of any of the following:

o Difficulty communicating and therefore being intimate.

o Major weight problems, including both too fat and too thin.

o Bizarre sexual behavior.

o Controlling behavior.

o Anger, aggression, or major mood swings.

o Inability to handle problems, conflict, or difficult situations.

o The need to create drama, attention, or sensationalize everything.

o Fear of commitment, or desire to commit too fast.

o Insecurity, possessiveness, mistrust, or jealousy.

Again, depending on the kind of abuse, this man may need years of intensive therapy. You're on a first, second, or third date here. Why is he even bringing up the fact that his uncle abused him? You're not committing yourself to a lifetime of hell trying to help this poor soul recover from his childhood. Even if you could, which you can't, he'll only come out the other end resenting you and thinking of you as his mother. You know, the one who didn't love him right the first time. You're not his mother, and you're not his shrink. Pick up your purse and move on.

DIANE SAYS: Pleasant, relaxed, comfortable, and familiar are all words that should describe your relationship. Dramatic, agonizing, painful, and obsessive are all words that belong on CNN, not in an email you send to your girlfriend describing the last time you were on a date with a man you met online.

Now that you're fully equipped with the information you need to weed out a few major psychological problems, let's talk about money.

Your ride's pimpin'. His ride's gimpin':

You show up in a BMW, and he shows up in a rusty Corolla. Trust me on this one. Unless this dude is THICK11 and actually has the self-esteem to go along with the package, this isn't going to work. This section is not about being a snob. It's about obvious disparities in income. If it's noticeable on the very first date, it'll be noticeable on every date, and trust me when I say it's not something a good man will be comfortable with for long. Note that I said a *good* man will not be comfortable with it for long. I didn't say every man. If rusty Corolla dude seems to have his heart in the right place, go ahead and give it a whirl. You never know. He might be one of those millionaires who does it to disguise the fact that he has money. Probably not, but check it out anyway. If he's the guy who turned wrapping burgers at McDonald's into Manufacturing/Operations on his profile, he still might be a great guy. You'll just have to see.

Just to be clear, I'm not talking about differences of ten thousand dollars a year or less in annual incomes. Those can be barely noticeable. I'm talking about differences of twenty thousand dollars a year or more. Let's face it, twenty thousand dollars, after tax, can make the difference between a nice two-week vacation in a four star in Mexico every year and a long weekend in a tent.

If he pays child support for one or more children, then don't forget, the difference will be even bigger.

The hardest part about dating a man like this will be ending the relationship when it doesn't work out. Even though you may be compatible on many levels, large differences in income always end up being a problem.

Why does it have to be that way? you ask. It just does. It's how men are programmed. They need to feel like men. Cavemen. The guy who goes out, hunts and gathers, and brings home the bacon. If he can only afford Spam, there are only two ways this can go. You can become the next great lover of SPAM—barf!—and never eat bacon again, or you can keep looking.

Trust me, I agree. It's a horrible fact of life, and it shouldn't be this way, but, girlfriend, it is. And it's best if you realize this and keep your eyes open right from the beginning.

Okay, now that we've uncovered all kinds of bombs that will cause relationships to explode, let's remember our vows.

Diane, I am looking for a real relationship. Therefore, I promise I will not:

☐   Settle for a man who has to ask, "Was I really that disgusting?"

☐   *Settle* for any man. I know that if I'm involved with Mr. Wrong, I'll never find Mr. Right.

☐   Make a decision with my crotch, not my head.

☐   Turn into Cinderella's sister and try to squeeze my big-ass foot into a tiny glass slipper.

☐   Choose to ignore the defects.

☐   When it's raining red flags, pretend that it isn't.

☐   Be any man's counselor, shrink, psychiatrist, or support group, unless I really am one, and he's paying me for my services.

☐   Become the next big lover of Spam.

Your autograph please:

_____

First dates can be hell, but you got through it. You think you found a PWP, but it's hard to tell. You both left the coffee shop with a promise to connect next week. What now? Turn the page, and let's keep clickin'.

CHAPTER 6

DROPPED HIS BALLS: NO FIRST-DATE FOLLOW-UP

But I liked him: Now what?

The first encounter was great. He looked like his pictures, and you felt the chemistry. He was interested in you and listened to what you said. He didn't show up in a '79 Corolla, talk about the size of his dick, or down a six pack before the appetizers arrived. You both agreed you'd like to see each other again, and you left the restaurant thinking, *finally!*

No emails, no calls, and a week later, you're wondering what went wrong. Because you read this book, you did not email or call him. You simply went home and waited for your caveman to return. Boy hunts girl down.

Okay, first you have to realize that whatever is preventing him from following up with you, probably isn't about you at all. If you posted up-to-date photos as I told you to, then he knew what he was going to see when he met you. If you had at least one conversation on the phone, he'd heard your voice and knew you didn't sound like Minnie Mouse. If he offered to pay for dinner, and you let him, that's not it. If he didn't offer to pay for dinner, but you offered to pay for your own, and you did, then that's not it either. There could be any number of reasons why Mr. Promising dropped his balls. These are the most common:

• <u>Chemistry</u>. Just like you, he has to feel it in person.

• <u>He's already in a relationship</u>. Married? Maybe. They aren't always easy to spot on the web site, or the first date. Some guys, however, aren't married but are living with or emotionally involved with a woman. Chances are that relationship is on the rocks. I believe these men go out on dates with women simply to make themselves feel better. They want to have options if they need them.

• <u>He got "scared off" by your BMW</u>. Remember the pimpin' gimpin' thing from the last chapter? Well it's true. If anything you drove, wore, or said made him believe there is a substantial difference in income, that can be enough to send some men packing. Here's the thing, men have to believe they will be able to make you happy. If you plop your Louis Vuitton on the table, and tell him it's not a fake, the first thing that's going to go through his mind is, "Oh man, I can't afford stuff like that." Translated from man-speak to woman-speak means, "Oh man, I won't ever be able to make her happy." If you're lucky he won't have a clue who the designer is or what the bag is worth. My advice? Don't enlighten him.

- It _was_ something you said or did. For every joke I make about the antics of men who participate in online dating, there's a man who can tell me about the crazy things women do. Now that we're on that topic, let's go into more detail.

These ten rules are simple. Memorize them. They are your what-not-to-do rules for your first, and some apply to any date:

1. Don't be early, don't be late. Just be on time. We're not playing games; we're finding love.

2. Don't interrogate him. Firing question after question at him about his profile answers, previous relationships, or job isn't the way to go. He's not at an interview, nor are you from Interpol.

3. Don't talk about you, you, and only you. It's a major turn-off for any guy. A good measure is to keep track of how many sentences you start with the word "I." You're allowed one every fifteen minutes.

4. Don't talk too loud. This one's easy to figure out. Nobody likes an embarrassing big mouth.

5.   <u>Don't talk too quietly</u>. This reminds me of the "low talker" episode on Seinfeld. It didn't work for her, and it's not going to work for you.

6.   <u>Don't talk about your pet for more than three minutes</u>. Unless the dude is specifically expressing sincere interest, it should be something you mention, not something you talk about for hours. You know he's interested because he keeps asking you questions not because he *isn't* falling asleep while you are blathering on.

7.   <u>Don't drink too much</u>. If you need to know why, have your girlfriends videotape you next time you're drunk. That should tell you everything you need to know.

8.   <u>Don't blatantly come on to him</u>. You know what it's called. Too much too soon. It's okay to flirt, but pawing at a guy who hasn't even attempted to touch you yet, is beyond uncool.

9.   <u>Avoid sex talk</u>. There's no reason to go there. If the dude wants to know whether or not you shave your pussy, and you haven't even had dessert yet, you should be walkin', not talkin'.

10.   <u>Don't turn him into your therapist or your daddy</u>. Avoid deep conversations about your rotten childhood or dysfunctional family. Let him find out everything that's great about you, before he finds out all the other stuff. It's just better that way.

How to GET a Second Date, and Other Bad Advice for Women

I'm going to suggest you *not* take advice from anyone who hasn't actually lived the online dating nightmare themselves. All kinds of experts and websites claim to be geared toward the internet. The problem is if you haven't been in the trenches, you really don't understand what it's like. Trust me when I say, it didn't take me long to figure out why all this advice was free. Honestly, if I have to watch one more uTube video that has a twenty-something-year-old overly cheerful, 125-pound, married chick saying, "Use a catchy profile name," or "Don't be nervous when you meet him for the first time, just be yourself," I'm going to puke.

One article in a popular online dating magazine even went so far as to say, "Learn to read body language before you go." Come on now. Unless you already have an interest in something like this, and have been studying for some time, what are the chances? It's not even remotely plausible. Time to hit the dumb advice delete button!

I wasn't surfing for long before I found it. The mother-ship. The uber-bad, "How to Get a Second Date" article. As you might have guessed, I didn't even get past the title without thinking *wrong, wrong, wrong.* We, the women of *Click*, do not work at *getting* second dates. If we have a second date, it's because the man we met was interested enough to initiate one. We do not pursue men; they pursue us. Caveman rules.

Want more great *free* advice on "How to Get a Second Date?"

You do? Keep reading.

- <u>Relax and be yourself</u>. Really? Who else are you going to be? And it's not as if you can just tell someone to "relax," and therefore they will. Nerves aren't always that easy to control. I could agree with saying something like, "If you already tend to be nervous on a first date, I strongly recommend you don't indulge in a grande espresso before you leave." But telling someone to simply relax isn't going to make anyone's first date better. We are who we are. If you're telling someone to *be yourself,* and *yourself* is a nervous-on-a-first-date person, then that's the way it is.

We all know how this first date thing really happens. You're going to see a guy's picture, maybe chat with him online or by email a couple of times, then arrange a coffee date. If you're nervous, you're nervous. Trust me, that'll go away really fast anyway if the guy posted a picture that's ten years old and fifty pounds ago. If he's as handsome as you expected, then being a little nervous is probably healthy. There's nothing wrong with that.

- <u>Don't have a mental list of questions</u>. I completely disagree. How can you spot the defects and return the goods, if you don't? You absolutely *should* have a mental list of things you want to find out about a guy you've met online. It's how you incorporate your questions into the conversation you need to be mindful of. If you simply fit them into topics you're already discussing, naturally, or introduce them as a new topic if/when the conversation dies, you'll be just fine.

"If I remember correctly, your profile said you are in IT/Education. What do you do for a living?"

You should always have a mental list. After all, you need to know if a guy who didn't answer, "How many children do you have?" on his profile, has six of them.

• <u>Don't tell him you had a good time if you didn't</u>. Okay, sure, makes sense, but isn't this really about not leading someone on if you're not interested? I totally understand how you can have a good time talking to someone for an hour over coffee, but that doesn't mean you want to date him. I've had that experience at least 100 times. There are plenty of nice, caring, down-to-earth men out there who can carry on a great conversation. It didn't make me more interested on a romantic level.

The reality is there are no "hook" lines or perfect actions that will help you *get* a second date. It's all about the chemistry. As you know, Patti Stanger, Millionaire Matchmaker always says, "The penis does the picking." You can tell him you had a great time, nice time, perfect evening, take your choice. The reality is, if the penis didn't get off the couch, he isn't going to call you. Period. Move on.

Note to my online dating magazine friends and *experts*. You really have to have lived it to know how it works.

Christmas party dude, my personal tale of woe:

I drove to a really good outlet mall just outside of Seattle to meet him. The beauty of arranging a date in a location like this is, if it doesn't work out, you can always indulge yourself at your favorite stores. Nothing beats picking up a new Juicy Couture handbag for half price. Nothing except a really great first date. Which mine was not. But it wasn't bad either, and since I take my own advice, I decided he was good enough to hang out with for the rest of the day. We'd talked on the phone a few times before I went down. The plan was to meet, and if we hit it off, we'd go to his company Christmas party together that night. After a few hours of talking and shopping, I decided to give it a whirl.

The moment we got to the parking lot, however, I knew we had a problem. Why? Because that's when I found out Christmas party dude was actually a rusty Corolla dude. Darn. Okay, my car's way better. It's noticeably newer and nicer than his car. Does this matter to me? No. Does it matter to him? Yes. Even if the guy doesn't say anything to you, just know that it does.

We proceed with the plans, and he follows me to my hotel so I can get changed. A couple hours later we were at the party. Did I drive? Yes. Why? Because it's the safe thing to do. I wasn't about to jump into the car of a guy I had only met that morning and head out to some golf course in the middle of I don't know where.

The party was about what I'd expected. He didn't get drunk, act like a fool, or do anything to cause me to believe I was only there to make the office secretary jealous. We went, we ate, we laughed, and then we left. Not really wanting to end the night at 11:00 p.m., we decided to go bowling, which turned into a competition and a lot of fun. The evening ended with a quick hug and a peck on the cheek in the lobby then I sent him on his way.

Did I care that he had a rusty Corolla? No. I enjoyed the evening and definitely would have gone out with him again. I might have even decided to have sex with him, but I just had that feeling. That…hummm, I-don't-think-he's-going-to-be-able-to-deal-with-it feeling.

So what happened after that?

Nothing. My gut was right.

Christmas party dude couldn't handle it. Whatever "it" was. But I'm pretty sure I know. It's happened before, and it'll happen again. When it happens to you, don't be surprised.

It isn't always about things you said or did. It isn't always about your weight. Sometimes the date will end, you'll walk away, and you'll never know for sure. The only thing you should be noticing is—the caveman is not pursing.

Diane, I am looking for a real relationship. Therefore, I promise I will not:

☐   Forget. Boy hunts girl down.

☐   Enlighten men about the real price of designer handbags. Some things are best left between girlfriends and credit card companies.

☐   Put any man to sleep talking for hours about Bootsie my Chihuahua, and her new pink dress.

☐   Drink so much I turn the date into something that belongs on reality TV.

☐   Sign up for body language lessons, just so I can GET a second date.

☐   Worry, for even one second, about why Mr. Promising dropped his balls.

Your autograph please:

_____

No first date follow-up? Took a crash course in body language but still didn't *get* a second date? No problem. There's plenty more where he came from, and sooner or later you're bound to find a normal one…maybe…Turn the page and let's take a look at what *normal* really means.

CHAPTER 7

<u>"NORMAL" CAN'T BE DEFINED</u>

When it comes to online dating, defining *normal* as it relates to a guy is easier once you've gone through the process of elimination we've already talked about. After sifting through hundreds of men and purging all the THICK11s, alcoholics, victims, control freaks, sex addicts, and rusty Corolla dudes, you might, I repeat, *might*, have before you, a normal guy. We'll see. Keep reading.

Remember the three different categories of men I described before? Well it's time to pay those dudes a more detailed visit. After all, you've posted your ads, followed the caveman rules, responded not pursued, gone out on countless dates, spotted defects, and returned many of the goods. Now that you're sitting across from a guy who could be *the one*, you need complete the final step. Figure out which category of *normal* he fits into.

Mr. Right for One Night:

This guy is like a fantasy. He's perfect from head to toe. He's got a body that belongs on a fireman calendar, and lips you can't stop thinking about. Everything from the hair on his head, to the shoes on his feet is gelled, pressed, or polished. His car, job, teeth, and outlook toward life are all perfect. Is he too good to be true? More than likely, but that doesn't matter to you. You're probably not going to hang around long enough to find out, right?

I'm not, Diane?

No, and here's why.

The easiest way to determine if a guy you've just met falls into this category or not is to pay close attention to what *you* are thinking. These super perfect guys unintentionally have a way of stirring up your insecurities. After all, there's a lot to live up to, isn't there? If any of the following thoughts (or similar) enter your mind, you are probably sitting across from a guy who has the potential to be one thing, and one thing only. A Mr. Right for one Night.

- *Holly crap! He's totally hot.* If you think that, all women think that. Figure out how many women that might be, and you'll have determined your competition, and therefore chances of success in a relationship with him. If you came up with the odds of 2,000,000:1, you're probably close.

- *I wonder if he thinks I'm hot enough to be his girlfriend.* In reality this thought shouldn't even cross your mind. You shouldn't care, but if you do, that's going to be the problem.

- *He could be with any woman he wants, including someone 10 years younger than I am.* And more than likely he was, last night, and will be again, tomorrow night.

- *I better renew my gym membership.* You never think you're thin enough, do you? Me neither.

- *I wonder how many women he's dating.* Simple answer, lots.

- *Why is a guy like this online?* Put really, really big stars beside this one, my friend, really, really big stars.

If you're capable of it, go ahead and have a great night with this guy, but if you sleep with him, go home that night or first thing the next morning. You don't have time for breakfast.

Why, you ask?

Because he'll be busy. Guaranteed. Work, the gym, an appointment to take the car to the garage—the list of excuses is long, and some are even convincing.

Meanwhile, if you're standing there naked, wearing his shirt, and thinking about making scrambled eggs, slap yourself.

Why would I say such a thing?

To save you from the embarrassment and heartache of possibly being *brushed off* while you've still got that morning-after glow. Not the best feeling in the world.

As good as the night may have been, you need to stay in control. He pursues you, remember? It's easier and smarter to just get up and leave.

Excuse me, but *you're* the one with the appointment. Most women will unfortunately do the naked-cute-shirt-kitchen thing.

You, on the other hand, will be mysterious.

You won't be clingy, needy, or desperate. You will be the 1:2,000,000 women who gets up and walks away as if nothing happened.

You will shock the boxers off Mr. Calendar-bod, and he won't be able to stop thinking about you, and trust me when I say it won't matter if you're a 7 or a 10.

> **DIANE SAYS**: When you're out with this dude, don't pretend you don't notice that his cell phone is constantly vibrating with calls and text messages. No. No. No. They aren't from either his mother or the company server sending him status reports. I can't believe women fall for the server one, and I can't believe I've heard it so many times. Another sign you should watch for—the bathroom trips. Sometimes a man's only escape while he's with you is the men's room. It's the perfect place to answer emails and text messages to "prove" to other women he's alone. Be suspicious of any man who disappears into the washroom one too many times or seems to take forever while he's in there.

.

The point is, you want to have a good time, then leave the next day with your pride intact. If you see Mr. Perfect again, continue to manage him in the exact same way. Stay in control and try not to let your emotions get the best of you. Men who are that hot are online for a reason. Trust me when I say it's typically not because they're looking for a wife.

Borderline Boy:

You are with a borderline boy if you're:

•   completely   unsatisfied   with   your relationship   because   he   doesn't   support   you emotionally, he's never *there for you*, he's a liar, cheater, or anything else negative that you've been able to prove more than twice, but you stays in it because the sex is good, or because the sex is better than no sex; or,

•   you stay with him because you haven't found someone better; or,

•   you stay with him because you believe you can't find someone better; or,

•   you stay with him because you've got a super bad case of the *at least he's* and you've decided to give up and settle for this guy; or,

•   any combination or variation on the above.

The bottom line with this guy is that he hasn't added any value to your life, even if he's not necessarily taking anything away from it. He has never said he loves you, but he's never said he hates you either. He isn't going to marry you, but he isn't going to throw you out. Do you know what a borderline boy is in reality? He's a roommate that you have sex with.

Here's a creepier way of looking at it. You're only one small step above having sex with your brother. Ewwh!!! It's not good. A borderline boy has the potential to suck up the best years of your life then suddenly dump you for his hairdresser. You know the one with the tattoos who makes $10.50 an hour down at Supercuts. And get this. *She's* the one who'll end up with the ring. It won't matter if you have his baby either, in fact that will only complicate things when he finally does jump ship. You see, a borderline boy is doing the same thing you are. He's:

• completely unsatisfied with the relationship but stays in it because the sex is good, or because the sex is better than no sex; or,

• stays with you because he hasn't found someone better; or,

• stays with you because he doesn't believe he can find someone better; or,

• stays with you because he's got a super bad case of the *at least she's,* and he's decided to give up and settle for you; or,

• any combination or variation on the above, which will end with him not marrying you.

A Penis with Potential:

Big deep sigh. Finally. There he is. Normal. He pursued you, arranged the date and took you to a nice restaurant with the kinds foods that you could both enjoy. None of the waitresses knew him or winked at him when you arrived. He even left his cell phone face up on the table when he went to the men's room. The conversation was entertaining, and he was able to discuss at least one long-term relationship or marriage he's been in, without anger or resentment. He may have even mentioned how he's learned something from his mistakes.

When you're dating a PWP, it's obvious. He's into you, but he's not declaring his love for you after knowing you less than a month. You know in your heart that he's there for you 24/7 even if you don't really want him to be. Unlike the borderline boy, he's eager to introduce you to his friends and family. Every time you're together bells *aren't* going off in your head. It isn't raining red flags. A penis with potential is easy to spot because:

- He doesn't have *intriguing* problems. You know, the kind you actually have to research, psycho-analyze, then spend hours talking about with your girlfriends. Groan.

- He doesn't suck you into all kinds of (baby momma, psycho-ex, family dysfunction) drama the first week you know him.

- He simply shows up when he says he will. Go figure.

- He doesn't tug at your heartstrings by looking or acting like an unwanted puppy at the SPCA.

- He doesn't tug at your bad-boy heartstrings by looking or acting like an aloof, moody rock star who hasn't eaten in months.

- He demonstrates that he *does* have his life in order. He has a real place to live that you're able to go to, a real car that he is able to drive, and a real job that he can talk about.

• He has multiple friends and good relationships with most of his family, and you know this because you've met them.

• He is willing to discuss all aspects of his life openly, and what he tells you is true.

• **The most important one of all.** He is available when you call, and there aren't any toilets flushing or water running in the background. Remember they might say that *a good man is hard to find*, but in 2011, he shouldn't be hard to reach by phone.

They're not all going to be PWPs

As you know by now, I'm not exactly the advocate of "no sex until you're engaged," and I'm certainly not all about "saving it" for marriage. The reality is, you're going to meet a lot of men online, and they're not all going to be PWPs. That said, many of them will be attractive enough to spend the night with, maybe two. Not a problem. But before you get **temporarily** involved with any of these guys, you're going to need to know how to keep your head on straight.

What do I mean by that? It's simple. You need to be able to spend a night with a guy, have a fabulous time—which includes sex if you choose—and then be able to walk away the next morning and simply see it for what it was. Just sex. In other words, be a guy. Play like the boys.

Specifically, what I mean is:

> 1.   Don't believe that just because you slept with him that now you now have a boyfriend. Don't even begin to think that. He doesn't think he has a girlfriend, trust me.

> 2.   Don't *you* call, text, e-mail, phone, Skype, instant message, or in any other way try to contact him after the "date." It's his job to follow up. Your only role here is to decide whether or not *you* actually want to see *him* again. Caveman pursues, you respond.

> 3.   Don't sleep with your head on the phone hoping he'll call. Whether or not he follows-up is NOT an indicator of your self-worth. Not at all. You did what YOU wanted to do, and that's the ONLY validation you need.

> 4.   Don't talk about him with your girlfriends all day long. Stick with, "Yes, I had a great night, the food was good, the movie was good, the sex was good." Period. End of discussion. If they ask you what you're going to do if he never calls you again, the right answer is: "Nothing. I might also do nothing if he *does*

call. We'll see." Then grin, like Sharon Stone did in *Basic Instinct*. You know the scene.

A few words of caution. If you met a *normal* guy and have categorized him as a PWP, **you will not have sex with him on either the first or second date.** Oddly enough a normal guy who is truly interested in you won't find this to be a problem at all. In fact he may even expect to have to wait longer. That's a good thing.

Okay, you met KING4QUEEN, and you believe he's a PWP. It's date number three, and you're ready to get it on. Trust me when I say, after the deed is done, you're going to find out if he really is a borderline boy. If that happens, and as soon as you realize it, the next step is easy. You simply re-categorize him. There is no upward or downward re-categorization rule other than **it can only happen once**. For example, a borderline boy could turn out to be a PWP and be re-categorized "up" accordingly, one time. The same will apply to a PWP, "down" to a borderline boy. However, KING4QUEEN cannot be re-categorized back "up" again if, in fact, you discovered that he was really looking for a harem and forgot to put an "s" at the end of queen.

Bottom line. He is what he is.

Another triple-start note: If you've re-categorized him more than once, you have:

- Lowered your standards – Go back and re-read chapter two, do not pass go, do not collect $200.

- Oxytocin brain – The sex is good, but he drives you blinkin' crazy. Time to give your head a shake, girlfriend. The temporary highs are never going to be worth those all-time lows.

- Settled – The worst result ever. You've spotted the defects and are refusing to permanently return the goods. There's no excuse for this. To return the goods in this store a Click girl requires no receipts.

Diane, I am looking for a real relationship. Therefore, I promise I will not:

☐   Try to have a long-term relationship with any man who has me thinking that I need liposuction, hair extensions, and a personal trainer from Jackie Warner's team at Sky Fitness.

☐   Ignore the fact that super-dude has, for whatever reasons, resorted to online dating.

☐   Date any man who has been to a plastic surgeon more than I have.

☐   Believe that just because I had sex with a man, that I have a boyfriend.

☐   Forget the alternate use guys have for the men's room.

☐ Wrongly interpret a man without a hodgepodge of *intriguing* problems as boring.

☐ Forget that I never need a receipt to return the goods.

☐ Take unwanted puppies home from the pound unless they have four legs and a tail, in which case I'll be assured of unconditional love.

☐ Sex... brother... gross. No need to say more.

☐ Forget to practice my finest Sharon Stone grin.

Your autograph please:

_____

Now you know what the non-definition of *normal* is, and the three categories men fall into. Great, but don't go anywhere. We're getting to the good stuff. The next chapter is about getting naked. Turn the page and, as Salt-N-Pepa would say, *Let's Talk About Sex, Baby.*

CHAPTER 8

DRIVE THROUGH SEX: THE ART OF THE TEMPORARY RELATIONSHIP

To master it, one must first understand it:

I'm calling it a *temporary relationship* because we're not just talking about having a *one-night stand*. It might mean one night, but it could also mean two, maybe even six. Whatever works for you.

This is the kind of relationship you can have with either Mr. Right for one Night, or a Borderline Boy. You do this because you still want to live your life and have fun while you're looking for a PWP. You want to play like the boys.

The words sex and commitment don't belong in the same sentence:

Yes, I am going to talk about commitment now because you need to understand it from both the male and female perspective. Why? Because commitment is the precise word that is *not* present when you engage in a temporary sexual relationship. If you try to force, manipulate, or even imagine those two words together, you're destined for heartache. Think of this lesson like open-toed shoes after October 1. You just don't do it, and you don't even need to ask why.

We both know that you've had at least one relationship that's gone sideways because you had sex with a guy, woke up the next morning thinking you had a boyfriend, only to be horribly disappointed a day or two later. I've done it. Every woman I know has done it. Some I know are still doing it.

The sooner you understand that sex and commitment don't go hand-in-hand, the easier it will be to just have sex. As I always say, if there ain't no ring, there ain't no commitment.

Commitment phobia and the old triple-whammy:

We all know that men are reluctant to commit. They can get sex without having to marry. Hell they can get sex without having to buy most women a drink. They aren't pre-programmed to want children, and they certainly don't face the same social pressures to get married that women do. Not only that, they can walk away from a one night-stand feeling completely satisfied, tell all their friends about it, and be congratulated for their prowess vs. being called a slut. Must be freakin' nice.

Women, on the other hand, are faced with what I call the old triple-whammy.

> 1. <u>Gender influence</u>: This isn't a big news flash. However, we tend to forget how much impact it has on our lives. The fact is that you've grown up gender-influenced by what your parents, teachers, and preachers have taught you. Wanting anything short of marriage, three kids, and a home in the burbs is selling yourself short.

> 2. <u>Mother Nature</u>: If you're in your early thirties, you have Mother Nature working against you. The old biological clock, ticking away, telling you it's time, you're ripe. You have business to attend to. Whether you think you want kids or not is a different story.

> 3.   <u>Oxytocin</u>: Worst of all, you're wired differently than your male counterparts. Your emotional response system will almost always associates sex with love and love with commitment and fidelity. One good orgasm, and oh man, you are doomed. The "hormone of love," also known as

oxytocin is sending crazy-ass messages to your brain: H*e's the one.* But is he really?

What can I say? He's reluctant, you're not. You have good sex with him, and you're planning the wedding. He has good sex with you, and he's out looking to have good sex again, tomorrow night, with someone else.

That's nice Diane, but I already knew that about men.

Good. I'm glad to hear that; however, I think it's always worth revisiting. I've seen too many of my friend, otherwise intelligent women, forgetting about this the minute they get emotionally involved with a man. How did they get that way? They slept with him and actually had an orgasm, a good one.

Trust me when I say, I'm not the pot calling the kettle black here. I've done this myself. In fact I've done it so many times that I actually–finally–had to learn from it.

The point is, you have to remember that for men sex can just be that. Sex. They don't get the oxytocin rush from a good orgasm that we do, and suddenly feel compelled to start shopping for a ring. In fact, it seems that it mostly just compels them to go and find a woman to have another good orgasm with.

As you know, there are a million books out there devoted to relationships, love, commitment, and the male and female emotional response systems. You've probably read a number of them. Instead of diving back into all of it, let's review the major points relevant to this subject.

1.   Men are reluctant to commit.
2.   You want a commitment.

3.   Men don't always associate sex with love.

4.   Women almost always associate sex with love.

What's wrong with this picture?

- For men > sex = sex = sex
- For women > sex = love = commitment

These two equations simply do not align, and the grand conclusion here is, **having sex with a man will not guarantee you will end up with (a) a boyfriend, (b) love or (c) commitment.** In fact, most of the time, it will not result in any of those things.

All this means is you really need to start thinking about sex in a different way if you're online and don't want to sit at home and dry out while you wait for your perfect PWP. Seriously girlfriend, it's time to level the playing field. It's not 1957 anymore. *Leave it to Beaver* is off the air. Miss Manners has left the building. Men don't worry about what other people will think if they have a temporary relationships with women. So why should you?

Life after sex:

One good orgasm and you can feel like you're in love. Whether you really are, or should be, is a completely different story.

You *can* control this. If you want to have successful temporary relationships, while you're still looking for your PWP, all you have to do is **control your thoughts**. Remember, you have determined that he was either Mr. Right for One Night, or a Borderline Boy, in other words, good enough, for now. You have also determined he was *not* a PWP, and therefore *not* good enough to be the father of your children.

So…after a great night of sex with KING4QUEEN, recently downgraded to a Borderline Boy, the first thing you have to do is pay attention to your thoughts. Don't let yourself get caught up thinking about the ring, the dress, and the song you'll play for the first dance. <insert sound of needle screeching off the old vinyl record here> Instead, think about shitty diapers, a loser sitting on *your* couch who hasn't washed a dish in weeks, and the unpaid electric bills stacking up on the counter. Maybe top that off with a half empty six pack of beer, a backwards baseball hat and a few of his buddies watching WWF. That'll end that whole romantic fantasy real quick. Here's the thing. You know as well as I do that the backwards hat scenario isn't that far off what you, or someone you know, has experienced, or is experiencing now. Trust me. Good sex is rarely worth it. Don't settle.

The association you make between sex and love isn't the same association he makes. One good orgasm for a man, and he's happy. That's all, happy. No wedding bells, no diamond rings, just happy.

It was a great night for both of you. There are two ways this can go. He calls, or he doesn't call. If he calls the next day, fine. Do whatever you feel. If he calls more than three days later, you know immediately that he's nothing more than a Mr. Right for One Night and you proceed with caution.

Since we're talking about life after sex, please, please, please, if you understand one thing from this entire chapter, understand this. **Whether or not KING4QUEEN ever calls you ever again is in no way an assessment of your self-worth.** Do not, I repeat, do not give that power to someone else. Whether or not a man calls you after you had sex with him is not a judgment of how beautiful you are, whether or not you were good in bed, or whether or not he thought you had fat thighs. It is not an assessment of whether or not you are loveable. His response can only become something negative **if you make it that way in your head.**

You will not:

- THINK about him and whether or not he will call.

- THINK about all the negative things your friends and/or family might say if they knew what you did.

- THINK of him as anything other than a stepping stone on the path to your perfect PWP.

- THINK about him at all.

- THINK anything but positive thoughts that work for *you*.

No, I'm not crazy. Stay with me for one more second.

Ever heard of visualization techniques? Ever heard of the law of attraction? How about The Secret?

Feeling good, feeling loving, and visualizing are all very fundamental parts of creating the life you want. Don't stop yourself from enjoying something that will help you tap into those feelings and put you into the state you desire. You need to know how it feels if you want to have it.

After a great night of sex with KING4QUEEN remember to control your thoughts. Don't think about *him*, think about *you*. Remember the nice things he said. How soft your skin was, how beautiful you were. Tell yourself he was right. Convince yourself that he was right. Then add the feeling to it. Focus any soft, loving feelings you have on yourself instead of him. Be okay with feeling love for yourself. Let yourself feel happy and sexy. Remind yourself over and over again how good it feels to be sexually desirable. Then think about your perfect PWP. Have your romantic fantasy. Just, whatever you do, don't make KING4QUEEN the groom in that picture. See what I'm saying? If you're having a hard time coming up with a generic groom, insert the face of your favorite movie star. The point is, be dreamy all you want. Just don't be dreamy about the wrong guy. Focus on you. Besides, what's the worst case scenario here? Johnny Depp shows up on your doorstep?

If you turn the great night of sex into positive mental visualizations and feelings about your perfect PWP, that's what is going to help you find him. It will help you create the life you want more than any online dating site, more than any well-worded profile, more than a great picture, and definitely more than any checklist of dos and don'ts that anyone can create for you.

That's great, Diane. I get what you're saying.
I'm glad you get it. Why am I sensing a *but* here?
Because there is a but. *A whole bunch of* buts, *like*:

- *But why didn't he call?*
  - Who cares?
- *But he said he'd call.*

    ○ Again, who cares? We all say things we don't mean. They're called "little white lies." Don't take it personally.

- *But he told me I was beautiful.*

    ○ You are. That's all you need to THINK about.

- *But it was such a great night. You'd think he'd want to do it again.*

  o   Yes, it was a great night. Just focus on that.

- *But what if I can't control my thinking?*

  o   You can if you want to. Period.

- *But what if my friends think I'm a slut.*

  o   Don't tell your friends, or get new friends, or buy your friends this book. The bottom line is, a real friend will understand.

- *But isn't it selfish to only think about yourself?*

  o   If you won't give to the poor when you have more than enough to do so, then yes, you are selfish. If you have a great night with a guy and afterwards focus on how good it made you feel, that's not even remotely selfish. I don't believe you can ever be too selfish when it comes to supporting your own self-esteem and self-worth.

Got any more excuses for why this might not work?
No.
Good, let's keep clickin'.

Diane, I am looking for a real relationship. Therefore, I promise I will not:

☐   Forget that whether or not a man calls me the next day is **not in any way, shape, or form an assessment of my self-worth, beauty, or whether or not I am loveable.**

☐   Live in the past. 1957 is over, and there aren't a whole lot of things worth going back there to get, including cloth diapers, sanitary pad belts, and nylon stockings without Lycra.

☐   Forget that for men sex = sex = sex. Nothing more. No ring, no dress, no white picket fence.

☐   Believe that just because I had an orgasm with a man, that I am in love with him. I know it's just the oxytocin talking.

☐   Expect to **get** a boyfriend, love or commitment in exchange for sex.

☐   Forget that playing like the boys means commitment (just like batteries) not included.

☐   Settle. Put the wrong groom in the picture and end up with a loser on *my* couch.

Your autograph please:

_____

Temporary relationships and long distance relationships have a lot in common. What if the next promising email comes from a guy in Hawaii? Beautiful place, but...

Don't worry. Turn the page, I've got yah covered.

CHAPTER 9

LONG-DISTANCE DILEMMA

L ong-distance relationships have their pros and cons. What's great about them is that every time you're together it's like a honeymoon. Well, if you're with the right guy it is. If you're not with the right guy, then a different "H" word comes to mind. Yes, I've had both experiences, and the second one is *not* fun.

On whose budget?

Meeting a guy from out of town is cool, especially if he really is a PWP. But unless he can afford to travel, it isn't going to work. I know, I know, but that's just the way it is. Remember Rusty Corolla Dude and how it really wasn't about the car? Well the same thing applies here when it comes to money. If he can't: (a) always travel to see you, (b) pay for you to travel to see him, or (c) cover the costs of at least half the travel, then it's not very likely the relationship will work out. If you're always the one shelling out the dough, it's just a matter of time before it wears on his pride, and if doesn't, trust me, you have other things to worry about, like (hint, hint), maybe he actually isn't a PWP.

Distance is the liar's best insulation:

The thing about the Internet is that men (and women) can be whoever they want to be. One "slip of the click" in cyber-world and, oh look! Suddenly he's: 6'2" single, never married, no kids, a real estate developer with an income of $75,000-$100,000. He has an athletic body, loves long walks on the beach, dogs and going to movies. The perfect man. In other words, anything he needs to be in order to attract you.

The problem, however, is three-fold. First, the guy who'll lie and say he's not married and doesn't have kids, when he does, will also lie about how many women he's dating, and the truth about who he *really is* won't come out for some time. Meanwhile you'll be investing your time, money, and emotions into Mr. Perfect until one day when your cell phone rings while you're sitting in the boardroom at work, minding your own business.

Hey, that sounds like it happened to you, Diane.

You're right. It did. Back to the point.

Eventually you'll get the call, and regardless of whether it's the other girlfriend or the wife, she'll be wondering who *you* are and where *he* was last weekend. If you don't get this call, then let's not play coy, we both know you're the one making it.

Yes, of course, not *every man* on the Internet does this; however, if long distance is a factor, you're going to have to watch for the clues, and follow your instincts a hundred times more than you would if he was local. Think about it. Why isn't Mr. Perfect, considering how perfect he is, capable of meeting someone in Los Angeles, Dallas, or Atlanta? They aren't exactly small towns. Why is he winking at you up there in Nowhere, Montana?

Things to keep in mind if you plan to start a relationship with what you perceive to be a long PWP. Oops, I meant long-*distance* PWP:

No you didn't, Diane.

I know. I wanted to make you smile.

Moving along.

1.   He probably isn't perfect at all. Let's face it, nobody is, and there's the possibility that some of things on his profile are lies, even the pictures. Tip: Chat with him on Skype (or any other form of Internet communication that allows webcam). Don't just pay

attention to him. Check out what's going on in the background. Can you see pictures, clothing, bedding? You can tell a lot about whether or not a man lives alone by his bedcovers. Think about it. How many straight single men do you know who own a floral duvet cover. Oh, and don't be tempted to fall too quickly for, "My sister bought it for me," or "I had that back when I was married. I just never bothered to get a new one." They are both highly unlikely scenarios, and the second one is even a bit creepy. Do you want to sleep there? I didn't think so. Also, make sure your radar is on if it seems like he can only chat with you (on webcam) when he's at work or at very specific times of the day or week. "Saturday mornings are best." Why? Because that's when the wife takes the kids to swimming lessons?

2.   Arrange the first hometown visit to occur as soon as humanly possible. Ideally, this is *you* going to see *him*, with him paying for all of it or half of it. This isn't a violation of the caveman rules because you will have left it up to him to initiate the contact initially, AND the idea of meeting in person. Making arrangements to meet is different. You aren't pursing, you're responding, and it just so happens, in the way that works best, for you. Why is it better for you to go there first? Well, it goes like this. He flies 350 miles to meet you. He walks into the airport, and you (a) fall in love, or (b) immediately think, *Oh crap. Now I have to*

spend the whole weekend with this guy, and he isn't half of what I expected. Trust me I've done (b), and it isn't fun.

But if I (a) fall in love, that's great, isn't it?
No. Not if you want a PWP.
Why?
Because you have no idea whatsoever who you just fell in love with. You can have a wonderful weekend together at your place, even end up in bed together. The problem is, now you're emotionally attached to this guy, and you don't even know if he has a floral duvet cover or not.

See what I mean? Not good.

Then, depending on what he has going on in his life, it could be a month or more before you see him again.

You don't know if he's flying from your hometown to BIGTITTYKITTY'S hometown then going back to LA or what the heck he's doing. The sooner you get on his turf, the better off you'll be.

You'll be able to see where he lives, what kind of underwear is on the floor, who lives next door, and whether or not she's giving you the evil eye.

Diane says: When you travel to meet a man, *always* ensure your personal safety. It doesn't matter how many times you talked on the phone, emailed, or "Skyped." Stay at a hotel until you really get to know him, in person. Make sure you leave contact information, including his full name and address, with friends or family. He should have no hesitations at all about providing this information. If you can't afford to go see him and stay in a hotel, you should not be pursuing a long-distance relationship. It's just that simple.

3.   A lot of websites will do a background check for a reasonable price. This check is typically a compilation of information found in public records, and therefore is not illegal. Before you fly anywhere, and for somewhere around $29.99, it's a good idea to confirm at least basic information, for example: address, date of birth, relatives, other residents at the address, neighbors, phone numbers, stuff like that. Before you jump on that plane and fly to Miami, make some plans on your own. If you don't have friends or family there, check out the shopping areas around the hotel or nearby spas or galleries, whatever it is you like to do. Book yourself an appointment or buy yourself a ticket to a show. What I'm saying is don't plan to spend every single moment with him, and definitely don't expect him to entertain you non-stop. You're still accountable to the caveman. You must let Mr. Miami

pursue. Following him around 24/7 isn't the way to do it. You won't create any desire, and you may even wear each other out. You also don't want to give him the wrong impression. Let's face it. Spending a couple days together is going to give him a glimpse of what life with you could be like. If he's already feeling burnt out, too heavily relied upon, broke, or anything along those lines, it's pretty unlikely there'll be a second trip. It can be difficult to spend two or three whole days with someone you never met before, for both of you. Don't push it, especially if things are going well. Here's a good rule of thumb. Plan to spend one third of the time doing something alone or with someone else. For example, if you're there for three days, spend at least one day (two half days, however you want to break it down), doing something else. Nope, sorry, this does not include sleeping. Good question, though.

4.   What's your emergency escape route? Did you even think about it? What if he turns out to be a total jerk and you can't stand to spend a second more with him? What if you've spotted the defects and want to return the goods, just as we talked about earlier? Maybe he has anger issues and is beginning to scare you. Always, and I mean, always have a back-up plan. If you flew there, make sure you can change your return flight or can afford to change it. Don't stay anywhere or go anywhere with him that won't allow you easy access

to a cab if you didn't get a rental car. Always have some cash on you in case you need it for something, including bribing a waiter to let you out through the back door of the restaurant if necessary. Don't even consider traveling without a cell phone. The point is, you need to be safe, and you are the only one who is responsible for that. Think about it before you go.

I really don't have anything against long-distance relationships. I've had many of them. They can be a lot of fun and suitable for someone with a busy lifestyle who doesn't need or miss having someone around all the time. In order to do this well, however, you have to:

  1. be able to comfortably afford it;

  2. have a job that gives you the kind of flexibility and time off you're going to need to facilitate it; and,

  3. have the kind of self-esteem that can tolerate the fact that you don't have a clue what the other person is doing when you're not together.

If you're someone who cares about whether or not your partner cheats on you, then this probably isn't going to work. If you have children, then this probably isn't going to work. If you're going to meet Mr. 3 or 4 kids, never married, lives in Georgia, Texas, then it's probably not going to work either.

Diane, I am looking for a real relationship. Therefore, I promise I will not:

☐ "Do the rusty Corolla" and spend all *my* money travelling to see a man. I have my own pride to worry about, never mind his.

☐ Fall prey to the slip of the click, I will do my homework and make sure he is who he says he is before I get on any airplane.

☐ Take or make any calls to or from women in relation to where he was last weekend. I trust my instincts. If I feel the need to drink and dial, I'll call him instead and dump him.

☐ Travel anywhere without a back-up plan.

☐ Talk to any man with a floral duvet cover unless I've received a hand-written testimonial from his mother confirming that she's forcing him to keep it.

Your autograph please:

_____

CONCLUSION

Right about now you're probably wondering why the hell you keep doing it. What I mean is, banging your head against the wall. The online dating wall. Putting yourself through all the crap, over and over again. Flirt, email, phone call, coffee. Nope. Flirt, email, phone call, coffee. Nope. Meanwhile the weeks, months and years pass, and you wonder if you're ever going to find him.

Love. It's a compelling reason, and as a result, the industry continues to grow. Some of the larger sites even take the opportunity to saturate prime time television with commercials during the loneliest season for singles– Christmas. Promises of perfect relationships, romantic evenings, and the end of single-life make it a lucrative business. I keep thinking there just has to be a better way. Trust me. If I ran a drug company I'd be all over this, burning the midnight oil to come up with a pill that would solve this age-old issue. Nice guy? No chemistry? No problem. Take two of these and meet me for coffee in the morning.

Until my new miracle pill is available on the market, we'll have to keep plotting. In the meantime there's Tylenol for the headaches, and that will have to do for now. The main thing to remember is you're completely in control of how good or how bad the online dating experience will be for you. If you follow the steps I've laid out, it should at least be better than it was before.

One of the biggest challenges I think you're going to have is the sex part. It was for me. I definitely know how hard it is to walk away from a dreamy guy you want to spend the whole day with after a great night of sex. Unfortunately, I also know how hard it is to be floating on cloud nine, alone, because you believe you met "the one," only to realize a week later he's never going to call. For cases like these, Tylenol just doesn't cut it. My company's second pill will be the morning-after-great-sex pill. That's the one that will stop the oxytocin from flowing so you can see him for who he really is. Just a guy who wanted to get laid? Maybe.

Stick to your instincts. Now that you know the categories these guys fit into, don't waste your time on Borderline Boys. Not if you're looking for marriage. Don't fall in love with Mr. Right for One Night. Not if you're looking for marriage. Don't respond to THICK11. Not if you're looking for marriage. Most important of all, and whatever you do, don't overlook a Penis with Potential. He may seem a little boring to begin with. But like I said before, you never know, he just might have a really big dick.

Yeah okay, you're single, and it sucks. The entire world appears to be designed for couples when you're alone. Look at the great seat sale. Only $250 round-trip to Hawaii. Don't forget the fine print. *Based on double-occupancy.* Buy one appetizer and get the second free. For who? My dog? Look, just because major airlines and the restaurant down the street can't come up with some new marketing angle that will tap into those 50 million people online who are single just like you and me, doesn't mean we have to sit home alone every night. There's no need to become a born-again-virgin. In fact I think it's important to keep putting yourself out there, experimenting with a variety of men, and taking a few risks with your heart. It's character building, and it will help you grow as a person.

Whatever, Diane.

I know. It sounds corny, but it's true, and it keeps you out there. That's got to be better than becoming known to your friends and family as "the spinster." The second that happens your old Aunt May will show up on Sunday with the single preacher from the church across the river in a small town you've never heard of. Then what?

I'm not saying you make this a full-time job. Sure take a break from online insanity every once in a while, but don't give up completely. Giving up online dating is easy. I've done it at least ten times. Then, after months have passed and it strikes me that I can't remember the last time I had a date, I try again.

Doesn't *The Secret*, the law of attraction and everything else out there that's new age spiritual tell you to *act as if*? *Act as if* you just met your soul mate. *Act as if* you're taking a long walk on the beach with your boyfriend. The fact that he has four legs, a tail, and chases seagulls doesn't matter. *Act as if* you are married. Go out and buy the dress. Plan the wedding, Feel the joy.

Acting as if is one approach. Just like everything else in life I believe that if you really, really want it, you're going to have to do *something* in order to get it. There are many options, and online dating is only one of them. Matchmakers, lunch services, speed-dating, meet-ups, singles clubs, the list goes on and on. Try one, try them all. There's nothing wrong with that. You just never know. You could be on your way to meet FUN2BWITHROB when you notice the perfect parking spot in front of Starbucks. You manage to slip into it before truck guy does, only to have him jump out to confront you. Of course you yell back only to realize truck guy's got a rockin' bod. The next thing you know you're both sheepishly laughing, and making plans to get together for dinner on Friday night.

You never know when it will happen. You never know where it will happen. All you need to know is that it *will* happen. Keep the energy flowing. Let the universe know what you are looking for. Create and maintain a mental image of the perfect Penis With Potential. Don't give up on any of your dreams and don't *ever* let the frustrations of online dating make you give up on your dream of one day finding love.

ABOUT THE AUTHOR

Diane Roberts has more than 10 years' experience with internet dating. She first went online in 1999, hopeful to find the relationship she'd always dreamed of. Now more than 36,000 emails, flirts, smiles, and winks later, she's ready to bare it all.

A self-employed, professional with more than 15 years' experience as a business and human resource consultant, she's written countless technical reports and business documents for clients, as well as countless dating profiles for herself.

When she's not busy writing emails replies to THICK11 and BIGWILLY7, she's writing novels for publication.

Roberts currently resides on both sides of the border. Travelling from Vancouver, BC to Las Vegas, NV on a regular basis, she hasn't limited her dating to her own backyard.

Although her formal education is business related, she has experience in both the boardroom and the chat room. Working around the clock to achieve her goals may reduce the number of dates she can go on, but she never gives up on her dream of finding herself a Penis with Potential (PWP).